C000213613

Reverend Grey

**Grasp the jewel
that shines from the
ashes of deceit**

Elaine C Johnston

Reverend Grey

Copyright © Elaine C Johnston 2018

All rights reserved. No part of this publication may be reproduced, stored in a retrieval system, or transmitted in any form by any means, electronic, mechanical, photocopying or otherwise, without the prior written consent of   publisher. Short extracts may be used for review purposes.

ISBN 978-1-907929-81-6

Contact Elaine at: bornoffiremedia@gmail.com

Website address: bornoffiremedia.org

Unless otherwise indicated all Scripture quotations are taken from *THE MESSAGE, copyright* © 1993, 1994, 1995, 1996, 2000, 2001, 2002, by Eugene H. Paterson, used by permission of NavPress. All rights reserved. Represented by Tyndale House Publishers Inc.

Ip

Editing, design and layout by Life Publications
www.lifepublications.org.uk

I Wish I Knew How It Would Feel To Be Free

I wish I knew how
It would feel to be free.
I wish I could break
All the chains holding me.
I wish I could say
All the things that I should say,
Say 'em loud, say 'em clear,
For the whole round world to hear.

I wish I could share
All the love that's in my heart.
Remove all the bars
That keep us apart.
I wish you could know
What it means to be me,
Then you'd see and agree
That every man should be free.

I wish I could give
All I'm longin' to give.
I wish I could live
Like I'm longin' to live.
I wish I could do
All the things that I can do,
Though I'm way overdue
I'd be starting anew.

Well I wish I could be like a bird in the sky,
How sweet it would be
If I found I could fly.
I'd soar to the sun
And look down at the sea,
And I sing 'cause I know
How it feels to be free.

Nina Simone

3

Reverend Grey

Acknowledgements

I could fill a book to thank everyone who has messaged me, called me up, hugged me, fed me and provided tea, coffee and wine and lent me their ears. For those who have advised, helped and encouraged my journey through writing and got me started.

For all our counsellors, you gave us hope and you believed in us. Particularly you who gave me hours of your professional council free without charge or time constraint.

You know who you all are and from the bottom of my heart I love you and

'I thank you'.

Dedication

I want to dedicate this work to my family. To my husband for allowing me to print our story, and unite with me to rescue others from one just like it.

To my children, for your timeless, endless, bottomless love and support. For patiently allowing me to 'Zone Out', sit in a corner and write for months on end.

I know you thought I had a serious case of 'crazy' but said nothing while I continued to lose myself into a laptop screen, surrounded by tea, water and sometimes wine, all at once.

I love you all very much and all my grandchildren, my heart is full and you are my inheritance.

I am very honoured to call you all mine.

Love Mum and Mama.

I also want to thank David and Jan Holdaway of *Life Ministries & Life Publications* for taking me on and making this vision a real possibility. For unravelling the lines to find the core of my story.

Most importantly, I am thankful to my heavenly Father for absolutely everything. For giving me my mountains and carrying me though my valleys, which means I can honestly say – He is My Everything.

Reverend Grey

Commendations

A perfect storm – betrothal v betrayal. This is the powerful yet very vulnerable story of a secret-keeper, one woman's journey out of a web of shame and codependency, and it is one that needed to be told. It challenges the subversive nature of Internet pornography and its devastating impact upon relationships. I am grateful for the author's clear honesty and the research that underpins it, and hope that it will help many who are similarly trapped to find freedom.

Jacqui Jarvis, MBACP Accred. Pastoral Counsellor

So often it is out of the ashes that new beginnings emerge. The author's story is just such an example! It takes courage to write about such painful issues and I commend her. Disrupted attachment in early life profoundly battles with the redemptive work of the Holy Spirit. It is in the darkness of ignorance and secrecy that the enemy most profoundly works. And it is in the light of understanding and truth that transformation and healing begin.

W. J. Fahrer B.A. M.Div. (Counselling and Theology)
Lead Counsellor with Anchor Counselling
Ordained Minister with the Mennonite Church
and an Accredited Counsellor with the Association of Christian
Counsellors

Elaine has written a book that she never imagined she would write. It is one that I challenge you to read. Why? Because it is a shocking story that belongs on the fiction shelf and not the autobiography one. You will read it with disbelief.

It is a story of incredible deceit that has spanned more than 30 years. I guarantee you will have mixed emotions and find yourself repeatedly saying: "What about…?", "What if…?","Why didn't…?", "How could he…?" And for different reasons, "How could she…?"

A book of such honesty could only be written by someone who has suffered shocking loss of much of what she once had. Yet, even in that you will find her story is one of grace despite the tragedy. Elaine has written a bestseller here, not because of its entertainment value, but because it is a revelation of the power of deceit, the value of exposure and an ultimate warning to many.

Rev John Bullock, Senior pastor of the Gatehouse Church, Moshi, Tanzania; Founder and Director of Agape Life and the 'Into Africa Foundation'; Author of 'For God's Sake, Let's Reinstate Apostles'

With almost thirty years of pastoral and missional experience behind me, it is safe to say that the story you are about to read is the worst case of deceit and betrayal I have ever known and I've known a lot! Elaine's brutal honesty as she tells her story should be read by everyone who is either in leadership or considering it. Why? Because with the millions of leaders on earth right now, the Johnston's cannot be the only ones caught in the trap of pornography, lies and adultery. If we are to expose the enemy's traps, then books like this should be on every Bible College shelf in the land.

Debbie Bullock, BA Honours, (Applied Theology), Director of Agape Life and the 'Into Africa Foundation'. Leader at the Gatehouse International Church, Moshi, Tanzania

This book is not an easy read, but in my opinion it is a vitally important book for anyone contemplating a life in Christian leadership. This is a true story lived over thirty years by two close personal friends of mine. May it be a powerful challenge to us all, to walk ever in the light as we serve Him.

Kevin Peat, Regional Leader for Elim Churches in Scotland, North West England and North Wales

Preface

My family and I would not be suffering the loss and brokenness we're living through now if I had known twenty or thirty years ago about the varying behavioural patterns, forms, and characteristics, distinguished by the common denominator called 'pornography'; that it eventually controls the mind and soul, and then destroys healthy relationships if the person affiliated fails to sever the tie with all that is associated to it.

My intention throughout this book is to bring pornography out of the closet, to raise awareness and, as horrible as the subject is, to stimulate face to face dialogue on the subject, to remove the shame that is attached to this sickness for the innocent victims and families caught up in it.

There is no other addictive drug like it because it is so easily accessed, consumed and ingested in total secrecy and, with the availability of the Internet and social media, at little or no financial cost.

Due to lack of education of cause and effect or statistics, I had no understanding of addiction to pornography and sexual perversions. Or the drug type effect it has on the brain.

Had I known then what I know now I would have insisted without compromise that my husband take time out to seek medical and professional intervention to reverse his behaviour and learn ways to manage his obsessions and compulsions for internet promiscuity, chat rooms and other destructive and immoral searching habits.

Now, in 2018, information is available for everyone to have the facts available to them, to view, consider their personal position, and then equip themselves for future protection.

It is true that not everyone who views pornographic material will become addicted, just as everyone who drinks alcohol does not become an alcoholic. But it must be recognised that addiction to pornography, and the many levels there are of it, is a rising disease that is corrupting the minds of young children, men and women.

Throughout the chapters I refer to pornography as my husband's addiction and obsessions. His behaviour was not typical of what would be considered pornographic, as viewing images and films were not his primary practice, though images were discovered and films were mentioned in his on-line dialogue with others.

To expose the details of my husband's habits in writing would be dishonouring and unnecessary to the primary purpose of this work. They're there between the lines, to avoid them completely would not uncover the extreme immorality of pornography.

My sincere hope is that in reading this story, people will become more aware of the dangers and destructive effects of something that is infecting our society at so many levels and in so many ways.

Please read, be challenged and wake up to the dangers there are.

Elaine

Introduction

For as long as he lived in the Grey,
He avoided the darkest night,
But did not see the Brightest Day!

Over days, weeks, even months or years, erotica, in its depraved mood, will cower in the shadows. Then, when its mark is in the dark it will pounce to devour its victim and demand its reward. Exceeding all boundaries of reason and moderation, while confiscating choice, it will steal freedom and blind the eyes of its mortal to the truth that they are no longer in control.

The incomprehensible exploitation of my heart and mind, and the unquenchable thirst within my heart, finds me painfully aware of my loss as another woman lays claim the one who is my life's one and only love.

She did not have to steal him from me, all she needed to do was lure him into her design. Her enticements didn't inflict pain, instead they masterfully numbed his conscience then deceived his soul into believing he needed her. He offered himself as a bond slave to her every impulse and desire. The evidence of such is explained in further detail through the chapters of our years.

He lazily adopted a trust as a child enchanted by a fairy tale, then offered his head, hands and feet to be threaded like a puppet on a string, which has no ability to make a conscious choice of its own. The devious strings 'Delilah' pulled deluded the one who is betrothed to her rival. He closed his eyes in lustful desire failing to read the small print that warned him the lease will expire. One day he will become empty with nothing more he can give, nothing left to satisfy or gratify, the ritual of toxic self-indulgence.

I recoiled from the searing knife-edge of torment as I watched the life of my lover, my husband, slowly bleeding out from the heart that once beat in time with mine. At the moment he is the tired and empty portrait of a man who was once a larger than life character.

No one can rescue him from his extreme, self-demoted dishonour.

It distresses me daily that he was unable to prevent the risk of laying our marriage, our children and grandchildren on the line, in their reckless need to use and abuse each other, with what began for no other purpose but the shallow gratification of a worthless rush of lust.

As I uncover the long-time closeted secrets of my husband's private battles I do not want to allow anything but the truth, as I see it, any place in this work. I have been silently covering up for too many years, so this is the time to tell it as it is.

The events I write about really happened. I have no need to sensationalise, rather the greater need is to de-sensationalise, without undermining the extremity of what the Reverend's pornography and sex addictions, coupled with my naïvety, overprotectiveness and fears, led us to.

You may or may not share our Christian faith, or practice any faith at all. If you have picked up this book and you are not a Christian, I am not attempting to turn anyone into a Christian disciple, or follower of Jesus. Christianity is the most non-threatening out of all faiths.

No man or woman can make anyone become a follower of Jesus.

The decision is made between God and a man or God and a woman and you cannot be coerced into that decision.

Introduction

It is a supernatural process of transformation. It takes the will of an individual to surrender to God, seek His life changing forgiveness, and want to be His child and Him their Father and to follow Jesus, as Lord and Saviour. No one can do that on your behalf, you cannot be indoctrinated or brainwashed into 'new birth'.

Please don't allow my strong reference to our beliefs and spiritual experiences put you off. If I didn't include these testimonials that underpin the personal foundation for our lives, our marriage and vocation, I would only be telling half the story. It is essential to make certain everyone understands that the vast polarisation between the very wonderful and the very rueful expressions of my husband's two characters was actually possible.

If you begin reading my story, please read it all before you pass judgment. You will read some awful descriptions of the deep scars that abandonment and rejection can create. Then consequently, how lies, deceit and betrayals arrogantly usurped authority over honesty and integrity with beguiling determination.

Most of all I want you to feel how very much I loved and still do love my husband. Also, I ask you to bear in mind as you read through each page how much I want him to rediscover hope over his losses, to then become the whole person he really can be and the father his family need him to be again. It is also my desire that many others will learn from our experiences and demise.

The circumstances I am suffering drive me to rescue as many people as I can out of the clutches of secret pornography and the temptation of casual sex before they, too, lose sight of their identity and surrender their chance of healthy, fulfilling and satisfying intimate relationships.

I don't believe my husband has ever totally established in his mind who he really is, due to reasons in his past over which he had no control. I pray he breaks out of the hallway of mirrors that he is trapped in. To be free to live the rest of his life, whole and complete, clean and united with God and his family.

This can only be his choice. He will need help, but the Reverend that he was, for now, declines the help he needs.

I have been privileged to be his wife, to share the life and love and the family we are blessed with.

I have known and loved my husband intimately for over thirty-five years, I know him better than anyone. The woman he is involved with has no idea who he really is. She only knows his darkness, his failures and weaknesses, the emotional and mental disability. His lies, deceits and betrayals are the person she knows. She has not yet learned that she will never win the war on his soul. He cannot escape the deep essence of the person he truly is.

Pornography is a rampant enemy of unrestrained, painful and cruel violations, which aggressively declares war on the mind and soul and does not cease, until every ounce of life has yielded to its intent.

Part 1

Breaking Point

I Miss – When you hold me tight,
Hugs in the middle of the night.
Making up after a fight,
And you say it will be alright.

This is a real love story of my husband and our marriage. True love stories bear little resemblance to fairy tales. They are relationships that love beyond pain, disappointment and heartbreak even when a 'Happy Ever After' is a long time coming, or never comes.

A very real enemy hijacked us. It wasn't the jealous Ugly Sisters, or Gaston the manipulative, selfish, charmer, or the wicked Cruella De Ville. I was unprepared for the fight and my husband was too weak. He was deceived, he didn't recognise the sinister intention of pornography until it was too late. We became the victims of an unseen and silent villain that we did not master, who infiltrated the doorway of our marriage with fascinations my husband could not resist. At that time it was the 1980s, our family was in infancy and the fear then was that we would lose everything.

I hate pornography; I hate adultery and I hate marital affairs. I hate lies, deceit and betrayals. I don't hate the people who get caught up in them, but I hate the ugly actions that cause terrible pain and I hate the great big mess those actions create.

More than three decades later, following the discovery of the most hideous and outrageous revelation, I had no alternative but to eventually separate from my husband of more than thirty years. He became involved with one of the women he met on the Internet. She served the drug to enhance a deviant appetite. Their shared discreet involvements brought them together to eventually engage in casual behaviours with no strings attached.

But of course 'No Strings' can ever be guaranteed.

I was not equal to my rival, the Internet, or her who my husband is involved with. It was not a fifty-fifty pursuit for his affections. I fought my hardest to win him back from the clutch of secret pornography and adultery. No human force, however, was strong enough to overpower the pillager who seized my husband's soul in her war against my marriage. One day, long ago, he took a fatal step into his secret world, and he was captured.

The cloak and dagger intrigue that secrets host only serves to increase the potency which will then become more and more seductive and destructive.

There is no such thing with addiction as *'The Status Quo'*. If you are in a similar situation, take my hand now, I'm reaching out to you. Let me lift you out of the bed of lies that has forced you into silence, that dims the light in your innermost chamber where truth sleeps. The cry for help is in your eyes, yet no one can see it. For your sake I expose the secrets of the immorality my husband engaged in throughout our marriage, of which there is no criminal law against.

Its roots trace back to immaturity and youthful sexual exploration lived under the self-imposed flagellation of silence for over thirty years. The whip that caused my tears and tore my soul to ribbons, enabled by self-medicated distractions, has been taken out of my hands.

Now I am free to talk about the relationship wrecking, marriage wrecking and home wrecking, invisible addictions, of lies, deceit, and the betrayals of marital affairs that began in the curious world of pornography.

I am not my husband's enemy, I am on his side, willing him to find the courage to challenge his addictions and fight for his faith and family, to be willing to stand with me so that together we can ruin the curse, to disarm pornography's purpose.

Men, women, whatever age, status or culture, who put on what appears to be 'The Perfect Life', then when you're inside the privacy and intimacy of your home, are embroiled in a sticky spider's web of lies and deceit that transgresses moral and civil conscience…*I am calling you now by name. Your name is Brave, your name is Strength, and your name is Priceless!*

We were not unhappily married. The cause of his unhappiness was his deeply damaged mind and emotions that produced a damning and addictive portal for sexual deviations to enter his mind and create a need.

I was never going to meet that need.

For too many years my husband stood with his feet astride betrayal and betrothal, managing to keep his marriage and family stable, until eventually he was unable to keep both feet sure. He was like a nation in combat against itself. When decency is at war with corruption, one has legal boundaries; the opposition is depraved in its greed to gain supremacy.

Win the battles it may for a season, but if honour and truth are brave, they will defeat corruption and win the final war! Secret porn incites a dark alliance that gets more and more sinister. The law of gravity makes no allowance for mortality once the leap is taken. Pornography is just as merciless and will remove all possibility of regaining a pure moral footing.

I fought as hard as I possibly could for my husband. In doing so I needed to maintain my integrity and morals, while she was posting photographs of her seductive nudity with sexual vulgarities, describing in fine detail what she wanted my husband to do with her body. These and many other messages and photographs spoon-fed his addictions, compulsions and disreputable greed. Such photos and messages from her would be sent to his phone while he was lying next to me in bed. Those are the charms he became powerless against. I couldn't feed his addiction like she did, instead I shamed it.

She may think she has won my place in my husband's heart. Her place is a very dark and suspicious one. Lies, adultery and shame are not a trustworthy framework to build a lasting attachment on.

> *She seduced her way into my husband's psyche, across the secret threshold that led to the dark side of his soul.*

Sadly, he wrongly thinks there is no way back for him at the moment. He has cut his family, and many friends loose to go ruthlessly, surrendered into the darkness of isolation and estrangement. Hopefully he will one day get this stuff out of his soul once and for all, to ultimately prove the brokenness and barrenness pornography offers and that it is void of love and respect.

He needs to see pornography fail him.

He has failed me too many times. No more, I now know the worst; truth in my life has been granted its freedom.

It is now time for pornography to fail him. Fail it will, however long it takes, at whatever cost to him and me.

My primary purpose is to make aware the unequivocal evidence of the destructive intent of secret pornography. I cannot keep quiet any longer, and secrecy of this sort needs a brutal slap.

Breaking Point

You're out there men and women, couples and families, with a history similar to mine. Living with the fear of exposure.

Sadly, there are also those who are already set up for a future that reflects our past.

I look back over the decades of my life and wonder, how did all of this happen in one marriage? The soap opera drama of our life's story went live on air, but it was not fiction, it was our real life. The consequences that were monumental unfolded year by year, and then month by month, now, day to day.

The groomer was groomed, and was too dazzled to run the other way and didn't have the mind, will or foresight to shout out for help.

I have a fierce sense of urgency to help those facing the same or similar punishing challenges in their relationships. If this is you hear me; expose the hidden concerns as early as possible. It will make no difference how many times a promise is made and sorry is said. If you're close to someone who is concealing their pornographic internet activities from you, they are in big trouble, and will need help. Remaining silent while accepting apologies and promises is loyal but it will not help either of you. It will be impossible to stop if pornographic stimulation remains undercover.

I am unlocking the trapdoor to our very private and personal cellar, where fear is the most loyal ally of shame, and serves as a padlock only to be opened by breaking silence.

> *The recklessness of the invisible destroyer escalates to demand its ultimate price tag — You!*

Beware of the Beast...it is devouring. It is never satisfied and will eventually strip you of flesh and breath if cloistered fantasy is relied on to feed addictions of illicit sexual arousals.

Time to reflect...

Are you are carrying a secret addiction or obsession, fascination or compulsion, either your own or for your spouse, partner, parent or your child or someone else? Are you internalising the worry and anxiety it causes you because the consequences of breaking silence will cause catastrophe and possibly the ultimate breakdown of relationships and loss? As a consequence of my husband's addictions I have suffered the loss of my home and career, finances and lifestyle.

You may need to get stuff off your chest, to pour out your pain and worry. You may want help, advice or support. Maybe you are surviving an exposure of adultery. I know how that feels from my many years' experience. You don't need to reveal your name or any other personal details. If I had been offered the opportunity to talk completely anonymously over the past years of my husband's secret addictions, it would have been a lifeline for me. I want to offer you a shelter where you will find someone who can empathise as you share your pent up pains.

I want to help you to manage your painful silence. You are not alone in your pain, you are not the only one. The most important thing is that you find a place or person to go to for support and prayer.

Psalm 34:17-20

Is anyone crying for help? God is listening, ready to rescue you.

If your heart is broken, you'll find God right there; If you're kicked in the gut, he'll help you catch your breath.

God is there every time.

He's your bodyguard, shielding every bone; not even a finger gets broken.

(The Message)

Setting the Scene

A note to self... Life is far too precious to worry about matching socks!

The therapeutic and cathartic process of unlocking the trap door of memories is a very necessary purging for the purpose of recovery.

The negative impressions that have left deep imprints on my mind have had squatters' rights for too long. It's time for a mindset makeover and a detox in my soul. I need to see and feel the insanity of it all, to re-establish my sanity. I need to see and feel the torment and anguish, to be capable of expressing, not suppressing, the assault and violations committed against our vows. His two identities were never supposed to collide. The one I call...

'The Reverend'

He was my husband; he was the wise one who I married. For now, he is lost.

The other I call...

'The Grey One'

The other woman has him. Grey is all he is for now and has been for a long time. He lives every day on the dark side of lifestyle choice; he is a fool, and he would admit that of himself. At the moment my husband is trapped almost totally in the Grey One's identity. How could the Reverend be the foolhardy Grey One? It was quite simple, because the Grey One didn't exist. He was a ghost identity, like an imaginary friend.

> *The name 'Reverend Grey' sums up the incomparable uniqueness of the two identities; the Reverend who was wise, the Grey One, a fool.*

The Reverend was also; Mr I Don't Know, Mr Maybe/Maybe Not, Mr I'm Not Sure, Mr Possibly/Possibly Not, Mr I Think So/I Don't Think So…I could go on. His indifference to what should have been very clear and decisive drove me nuts at times. He survived in an extremely wide grey area. This was the space where allowances for betrayals were made.

He would always *make adjustment to his choices, never judgement.*

The Reverend was very aware of the Grey One's wrongs. His grey area played to his vices. It is crucial to understand that the Reverend was indeed the real deal yet who confessed to being two people. It was the Grey One who was the counterfeit identity, the phantom personality that the Reverend concealed, but hopelessly consented to.

It is also essential for me to say, without excuse, that it was the Reverend who lied and deceived to keep the Grey One satisfied, while hidden in a cellar, dark and unseen.

The Grey One is everything contradictory. Altogether incompatible with the man I have known for a lifetime yet the two polarised identities are in one person, distinguished by opposing extremes in values and morals.

Following his exposure I was willing to allow the Reverend time to recover from his addictive lifestyle and affairs. I realised he would need patience; it would take time to rediscover our relationship and rebuild with family. I understood where his addictions were rooted. I knew it was not a reflection of how he felt about me and his family.

> *The unveiling of the Grey One became more frequent as the years passed by. His dark purposes and threats becoming ever more menacing, foreshadowing tragic and dishonourable consequences.*

If I had disclosed the Reverend's secrets to anyone I would have brought devastation to our house, our marriage, our family, our careers and callings. It would be as if I had activated a device that would begin the demolition process on our high-rise home. I couldn't be, and wasn't going to be, the person who did this. In faith I handed the responsibility of exposure to the will of a higher authority.

God, who sees all, knew everything there was to know about the Reverend and the Grey One. I resolved that if He chose to allow the Reverend to continue despite his double life, then so would I. If He forgives him, then so will I. If He extends grace, then so will I.

After more than thirty years of marriage someone, anonymously, uncovered the Reverend's secret scandals. This provoked the necessary outcome and painfully razed our house to the ground.

The Reverend was dismissed from his ministerial post. His credentials were withdrawn. He came face to face with the Grey One.

A duel that had been going on between the Reverend and the Grey One for more than thirty years escalated in intensity and became even more toxic that day. The Reverend was weak, he lost his authority, and then relinquished his rule totally to the Grey One.

Yes, our house needed to come down, but it did not require the ruins of our house to be brought so publicly to rubble, with such vengeful, cold-blooded actions.

The Grey One kept on taking over more of the Reverend's will. Becoming more painful and more destructive, he drained our resources and was never going to go away.

Pornography is an ogre, a personified man-eater. She ignores all boundaries. She is cunningly unseen and silent, and racks up more scores in her favour when ignored. If you are in a similar situation, begin now to rewrite the script for your future. Don't ignore the inevitable as I did. Give your relationship, family and possibly your career, the strongest chance to survive. Pornography needs to be forced out from behind the password on an internet device and brought into the daylight. I want to completely expose the nauseating and sinister molestation of pornography. To bring it out from hiding. The symptoms did not just affect the Reverend. They plagued and tormented our love and union. It disabled us chronically. We were both fighting it in our own way, but were unable to help each other.

In an unsuspecting moment one Friday afternoon I discovered chilling and shocking evidence that was again going to painfully and significantly change the direction of my life.

I knew I could not continue indefinitely in the cycle of betrayal, exposure, forgiveness, then to move on in pretence of trust. Nothing would change, so I had to.

I had enabled my husband's double life for too long. His enabler needed to step off the rug that covered the trap door to the basement of our shame. In leaving him I put an end to his real life, so the fantasy life can eventually die.

Time to reflect …

If you recognise yourself or a loved one in behaviours described above, take time to consider these questions, and then search your heart, soul and mind for your answers. Unless you are prepared to be honest with yourself, they will be of no benefit to you or those close to you.

- Have you ever had cause to question your mental health?
- Have you ever been accused of paranoia or obsessive behaviours?
- Does your intuition provoke uneasy feelings about the honesty and integrity of someone you are intimately involved with?
- On a scale of 1 to 10 how wide is your grey area?
  1-3: You stay very clear of questionable morals and criminal and civil indiscretions.
  4-7: There are occasions and circumstances where you feel it is acceptable to compromise on morals, values and minor laws.
  8-10: You regularly cross the line morally and legally. You let others down in doing so but as long as they don't know you don't think you are hurting them.
- Are you carrying secrets that are potentially harmful to yourself or others?
- Are you violating and betraying others by your unseen and secret actions?
- Do you fantasise about sexual promiscuity?

  Please take time to write down your answers to these questions and your feelings as you truthfully consider them. Write down the details and circumstances that relate to your personal responses.

  If you have answered yes to one or more of the questions, and or find yourself on the scale of 4 or above on Q4, find someone you trust to confide in. You cannot ignore these traits which care little for your wellbeing and will eventually eat you.

It would be good to pray this prayer, even if you have never prayed before. Give prayer a chance to allow God to help you:

Heavenly Father, I thank you that I can openly talk to you about these issues of my heart and actions.
You know me completely, nothing is hidden from you.
I confess I have wronged you, others and myself.
Forgive me and help me to forgive myself.
Guide me to someone I can trust to talk to.
Thank you for your love and forgiveness and help me from this day to choose to honour and respect (name those who you have violated).
Amen.

Psalm 51

Generous in love – God, give grace! Huge in mercy – wipe out my bad record. Scrub away my guilt,

You're the One I've violated, and you've seen it all, seen the full extent of my evil.

I've been out of step with you for a long time, in the wrong since before I was born. What you're after is truth from the inside out. Enter me, then; conceive a new, true life.

Soak me in your laundry and I'll come out clean, scrub me and I'll have a snow-white life. God, make a fresh start in me.

Bring me back from grey exile, put a fresh wind in my sails! Unbutton my lips, dear God; I'll let loose with your praise.

(The Message)

The Story Was Born –
The Handsome Gift of Fire

One child won't change the world, but for that one child,
His world changed, then changed again.

...**I**t was the mid-1950s.

A teenage girl became pregnant. This was not an acceptable situation for a single girl and her family in the country where they lived. The stigma on their reputation would be untenable.

A precious baby boy was born to this poor unmarried mother. There were no celebrations, greeting cards or gifts from family and friends to welcome this baby into the world. Messages of congratulations to the new parents didn't spread amongst the neighbourhood where they lived. No other choice was afforded to this young mother other than to hand her baby boy over to the local authority for adoption.

The grief in her heart must have sobbed violently, though quietly, as she hugged her son for the final time. She gave him his first kiss; her breath was the first scent to fill his nostrils. It was her gaze he first looked into when he opened his brand new eyes for the first time, as she named him Kenneth Theodore Mulligan.

She gave him very strong names, every time he heard them, he would hear "You are Handsome," "You are born of fire," "You are a Gift of God."

Kenneth means 'Handsome', 'Born of Fire,' Theodore means 'Gift of God'

35

He was set up to survive a hostile world because these great names of strength and surety would fill his mind moment by moment. Every day he would hear that he was handsome, that he was born of fire and was a gift from God. The mother, who painfully bore and birthed him, blessed him by name. Then, as a punishment for her moment of unrestrained and extravagant intimacy, relinquished her rights over her baby boy for the sake of honour and reputation.

He was taken from his mother's arms, from the most important person in his life. It was she who was equipped with everything necessary to provide for his wellbeing; the one important nurturer who he needed for consistency to form his first and most crucial attachment. The person who should have shaped and secured all his future relationships was gone, as if vaporised from his life. Handsome would never remember her, or anything about her.

He wouldn't recall the abandonment or how he felt to be in an unfamiliar environment with strangers. Unaware of the severity of his plight he would attempt to make that one vital attachment through communication as an infant child would. Then another child, possibly an older, more persistent baby, would cry louder for longer, so he would be overlooked again for possibly the ninth or tenth time that day.

The instinct of the child was to seek for what he was genetically designed to need for his healthy cognitive development. When a child is continually or overly exposed to stress it causes physiological alterations which affect the development of the brain. In other words, it triggers a malfunction that damages the potential of mental and emotional wellbeing. The calm composure of consistent regular attachment provided through a mother's or a specific other's love, along with food, warmth, eye contact and affectionate touch are profoundly significant in a child's most early days, weeks and months. If these neurological routes have been disturbed in some way, distress will be created in the emotional core of the brain that can then be affiliated to mental health problems as an adult, potentially causing depression, dissociative and other similar disorders.

Maternal and paternal instinct does not come naturally to all parents for varying reasons. It is a powerful force in most parents of a new-born, a strong natural desire that doesn't need to be taught. To want to hold their baby close and gaze into their eyes for a length of time that cannot be measured. To scoop them up into their arms for comfort, to reassure and console them to nestle in closer. Kenneth grieved those early building blocks to secure his mental and emotional health.

Kenneth, the wonderful gift of God, would possibly have cried out with his natural desire for emotional comfort for a few days, possibly he strived for two or three weeks, then would give up in his attempts to capture the relief he needed. A deprived empty void was formed in his mind where there should have been the psychological features forming pathological circuits in his brain that would become habitual sequences required for healthy attachments. All the solace he needed for his moral and emotional strength, as nature had intended for his sound security, was lost with his estranged mother.

Doubt, mistrust, isolation and insecurity were established as burial chambers in its place, infertile to any future growth from seeds of future attachments.

> *The unintentional damage had been done!*

This is my very personal, subjective opinion, due to my observations of children from troubled life experiences in their early childhood.

Females, broadly speaking, survive stronger than males. Females talk, they are in the main more open to embrace help and support and will persist in pushing the boundaries until they get what they need.

37

Males are generally more inclined to independence and apathy. Pride can be a very strong defence to anything that may be interpreted as weakness. Of course, there are many surviving males and many despairing females. It has to be recognised the historical trend that inherently men and women were shaped very differently in the past. Little girls would be hugged and consoled when upset, but boys would be scolded for crying. The cries of a cute, curly haired little girl would not be ignored.

Contrary to the theories that conditioned our culture in the early to middle 1900s, that hugs, tenderness and affection created weakness, is in fact that it actually makes us mentally and emotionally secure, strong and resilient.

Kenneth was not alone. Thousands of babies found themselves subjects of similar or even worse situations. Today they are possibly among our failing parents. They're our broken relationships, our lawbreakers and victims of addictions. Those who commit violence against others and self-harm their own bodies. Tragically some are convinced the only answer is the extreme act of suicide.

> *Sadly, yesterday's damage is done, set up to do its worst tomorrow.*

Now, in the early 21st century, babies and children in care are generally receiving the very best of all the emotional and mental support required for their whole needs.

Whatever the philosophy or beliefs of individuals, it is a proven fact that everyone needs consistent, strong and healthy, emotional attachments through infancy, childhood and adolescence in order to build good sound relationships necessary throughout life.

The family unit, however it is made up, at its best serves as a bedrock to secure the strong values and culture most hold important.

The Story Was Born – The Handsome Gift of Fire

For many different reasons young people turn to all sorts of addictive comforts to numb themselves to the consequences of circumstances they have faced.

There was a remarkable married couple, who were childless. They made inquiries about adoption, their request was to adopt a baby boy. Soon the good news they hoped for came; there was a baby boy, from a background of well standing. His name was Handsome, Born of Fire and Gift of God, in lesser words, Kenneth Theodore.

At five months old the handsome, born of fire, gift of God, Kenneth, was adopted and placed legally into the care of a loving Christian couple. This innocent child of only a few months old was reborn and renamed by adoption into his third attempt to begin his life. He was delivered into the care of those who would be his kind, loving and wonderful mother and father for the rest of their lives.

Research proves that the mind has its own memory. Everything that happens to us and everything we do from the moment our hearts beat, is stored in a memory bank of its own. It will all be remembered in our subconscious mind and carry significance through our entire lives, both the pleasures and the pains. In his subconscious mind Kenneth will not be forgotten, neither will his birth mother along with all the rest of the happenings prior to his adoption.

There is hope of restoring secure mental and emotional health from former damage, but it would require the purposeful intention of parents and carers to realign the young mind with many healthy, strong and consistent attachments. For an older child such as a teenager they would need to learn healthy coping strategies that subsequently correct the neurological circuits in the brain required for their stable mental and emotional well-being and attachments. As an adult the 'Handsome Gift of Fire' would be very generous with his sincere praise and appreciation for his parents who showered him with encouragement. He boasts of the love they gave and sacrifices they made for him. And rightly so, they were wonderful parents, who loved him unconditionally.

Due to his father's career path the family relocated many times. There were regular changes of homes, social circles, schools and friendships. The young man coped very well with moving around, due to the effects of attachment disadvantages forged in his mind as a new born. As a result he wasn't able to fully realise the effects of missing friends, houses and schools. Yet by consequence this lifestyle may have served to strengthen the silent fantasies of a child who needed to please. Once he had moved away he didn't remain in contact with those he would have considered friends, he noticed this trait in himself as an adult too. He also learned that being funny brought him popularity and acceptance. This skill continued as an adult, his humour won him warmth, like-ability and acceptance. What he never learned was that he didn't have to earn love, acceptance and warmth from those who mattered.

He liked school, particularly his boys' only grammar school. He admitted that he was caned many times for humorous, disruptive behaviour and would cry real tears laughing about his schoolboy pranks.

As he got older the double identity grew in creativity. The double life was forging its two diverse parallels. One that was near perfect, the model son, unless he was caught out, which he regularly was, the other one who would only come out in the darkness, not to be seen in the light.

Stories were humorously shared with many people, but were they the truth? I find myself wondering whether some of the funny stories that I have heard so many times over were not all fact. Were they embellished with fictional humour to increase the entertainment value, which would ingest his arousal for affection? Or were they the comedy of others that he plagiarised to gain the acceptance he was in pursuit of? Or were they the fake identity, the other one, who he invented.

Aged seventeen, and with his full agreement, Handsome found he was bereft of his mother, again, and in the care of more strangers due to his father moving with his work. Did this arouse and unsettle the deep tangible memories in his subconscious mind and the echoes of a baby's cry, from the long ago new-born? He wasn't a dependent infant now. He could go and get whatever he needed to fill the empty void of loss and loneliness. He couldn't have recognised that his mental health was scarred and disabled from unknowing neglect. It would be decades later when he would discover where his problems began, through no one's fault especially his own.

As a young adult living in a large city, there were many places he could go to find satisfaction for the anxious yearning within; easy access to top shelf magazines full of adverts of those all too willing to console the lonely with pleasurable, sexual, brief encounters, to then walk away leaving him emptier than ever!

At the age of sexualisation, which varies for each person, it is critical that the first experience is for the right reasons. It is so euphoric, it releases the desire for more, invariably the need will return to where it first sought fulfilment. I have suspicions that there are some undisclosed events around this time frame of his life that made room for his addictive flaw.

~~~~~~~~~~~~~~~

Very soon he found a career he loved in the Fire Service.

The baby Born of Fire became a Fire Fighter although even then, surreptitiously, the lurking *Grey* prowler was skulking in the shadows.

My husband told me the following events. As an experienced Fire Fighter the bells rang and off the Green Watch went to fight the flames in a two-storey house. A person was seen in the upstairs window. Up the ladder he went, without thought for his own safety, along with a colleague. Flames licked up the steel ladder, burning through his gloves causing third degree burns to the palms of his hands.

One following the other they jumped through the bedroom window, hitting the floor. At the same time a ball of fire engulfed the room. It headed for the window that a split second before they had jumped through. They had survived a 'Flashover'. With third degree burns that took the palms of his hands, his helmet melted into his face and burns to his ears he was rushed, with the other fire fighter to hospital. Remarkably the one I was to fall in love with told me he left the hospital within five days. He was prayed for by his minister who rushed to the hospital as soon as he heard the news. When visiting him, the minister had to be gowned and wear a mask to prevent infection, and could only stay with him a brief minute.

His healing was miraculous he would recount; new skin began to appear on the palms of his hands the day after the fire. He needed no skin grafts and has no scars. The new flesh that had grown on his palms was as soft as a new-born babe's. After a few weeks of convalescence, he returned to fight fires and save lives. He was presented with an award for his bravery.

He knew he could have died in that fire. He made his peace with God then shortly afterwards, left his loved career to follow a strong spiritual call to preach the Gospel and to go to Bible College.

The infant 'Born of Fire' was born into God's family through 'Fire!'

I later learned just how important those early years were in shaping the life and thinking of my husband and in determining the flaws that ended up costing us both so much.

(See Appendix)

Time to reflect …

Should you recognise yourself or someone close to you as a possible victim of neglect, rejection or abandonment, talk to someone you know will support you. It may be necessary to access counselling, through which the counsellor can assess your mental and emotional well-being.

You may have no idea that an early life trauma has affected you, but you will possibly find things begin to make sense. Why you react the way you do and other mysteries about some of your personality traits that don't appear rational will have a foundation of reason.

Pray…

Heavenly Father, you know me better than I know myself. You know everything about the circumstances of my life from conception until today.

You are aware of my birth and infancy and early childhood. Even though I cannot remember those months and years I ask you to return to any time in my history to heal my heart, mind and emotions of any trauma intentional or unintentional. Place a stop sign to all consequences of emotional damage that may have occurred.

I surrender all my worries, fears and insecurities that manifest themselves irrationally or unexpectedly into your hand. I leave them with you from now to dispose of them so that they will not inhibit me or hold me back from achieving my full potential.

I trust you to take care of my life, take care of my problems and difficulties from now on because you are my good and perfect father and nothing is too big for you to take care of.

Thank you,

Amen

Reverend Grey

Psalm 139:13-16

*Oh yes, you shaped me first inside, then out; you formed me in
my mother's womb.*
I thank you, High God—you're breath-taking!
Body and soul, I am marvellously made!
You know me inside and out, you know every bone in my body;
*You know exactly how I was made, bit by bit, how I was
sculpted from nothing into something.*
*Like an open book, you watched me grow from conception to
birth; all the stages of my life were spread out before you.*
The days of my life all prepared before I'd even lived one day.

(The Message)

His Leading Lady

It takes a lot of practice – to choke on fresh air,
Fall up the stairs, and trip over nothing.
I am highly qualified in all those skills!

I loved being the Reverend's wife. I love being a mum and a grandmother.

As a surprise to my parents I came along and was named 'Shining Light' 'Song of Joy' eleven months to the exact day after my eldest sister was born. She and I grew up like twins, though she always took her eldest sibling responsibilities very seriously.

We were very different in character, she was the sensible one, and I was the opposite. She was always clean and tidy and didn't like dirt. Dirt would fall on me; I have no idea how it happened. Within an hour of looking pristine, I would have a spare buttonhole at the top of my cardigan and a spare button at the bottom end, my socks would be filthy and food would mysteriously catapult from my plate to my clothes.

When we were old enough we would go to our grandfather's from school every day, then catch the bus home after teatime.

As a child, my elder sister didn't share the fear of strangers that I did. We were walking home from school together one day when an elderly gentleman shouted across the street to us for directions. My sister walked over the road to talk to him. I can remember being quite worried that she did that. I stayed on the opposite side of the road, thinking if he kidnaps my sister, I'll run for my life! Another time we were walking happily home, I had gone a few yards ahead. Suddenly, this very tall, stern looking, well-dressed man with a big black brief case ran with speed towards me. I screamed out loud and legged it for all I was worth back to my sister, who was completely horrified with embarrassment because the man was running to catch his bus and not running after me with intent to cut me up into little pieces and boil me!

I was part of a group of loyal friends, often spending holidays together, and weekends away too. We would chat and giggle until the early hours, day dreaming about our future and all our hopes and expectations.

There was a Bank Holiday Monday, we were all out together for the day, it was lovely weather, sunny and warm, and we were at big a park. A friend and I withdrew from the crowd for an hour or so. We came upon this lovely patch of green grass and decided to lie down in the warm sun. We set our jackets down to lie on, we closed our eyes and talked and laughed and just enjoyed the warmth of the sun. We had lay there for at least an hour, when a mature whiskered woman towered over us and said, "Excuse me girls, I need to get my ball in hole number nine!"

My parents worked hard and modelled a strong work ethic. They made sacrifices to enable them to provide for their four daughters well above their means. They modelled the importance of the Christian faith. They believed it was foundational to faith to belong to a local congregation and be involved in the church community. All of which led me to becoming a strong Christian as a teenage girl.

A Christian husband was my benchmark, I would settle for no other life partner. I longed to fall in love with Mr Right, and I was ready. I never imagined I had the qualities required to be a suitable wife for a Reverend, with my already keen interest in fashion and make up along with a nonreligious flair for design and shallow frivolity that I expressed through my own unique humour and style.

I am a Christian; I'm devoted to God, I enjoy fun, I can be dippy at times and also a little clumsy too.

I learned from experience how easy it was to become entangled in infatuations in the pursuit of love as a single young girl.

During the late 1970s and early 1980s I was a naïve twenty something single girl, having been sheltered well and taught good values.

Then I met Handsome, Born of Fire, Gift of God for the very first time...

A mutual friend introduced us. We only remembered this when we met again years later while training with many other young people on how to share our faith with others. Then we were divided into groups of three to go and put our training into practice on total strangers. I and another girl were teamed with Handsome and off we went to hone our learned skills on the passing unsuspecting public.

Despite him being good, I wasn't impressed. I thought he was a 'know it all' and he broke all the rules!

Following a life changing spiritual encounter in my early twenties I felt very strongly that I should apply to study theology. My sister and her husband to be were already part way through their second and final year of theology school. I travelled to the same college for my initial interview with a close friend who had also applied, our interviews were conveniently arranged for the same day. We made the most of our trip to spend some time with my sister. Handsome became part of the social circle while we were there – he was friendly, very funny and warmly entertaining.

I was accepted as a student and made arrangements to enrol the following September, along with my friend.

Reverend Grey

The week of the annual festival my family and friends attended every May was imminent. As expected, a crowd of people from my local church community planned to attend, a coach was organised, and we were booked to go. I was sharing accommodation with one of my sisters and two of our close friends.

We arrived, found where we were staying and got ourselves unpacked. On the very first evening, it was Saturday night, Handsome appeared. He stood out from the crowd. He chatted confidently and was friendly as first encountered. I recognised a twinkle in his eye and a lovable smile I hadn't noticed before.

His appealing personality became more evident along with his natural humour, he came back to my accommodation with his friend, they hooked up with my friends, and this became the social event every evening.

At the breakfast table on the Monday morning, he appeared, chatting to us as we ate.

He asked me if I would look after his keys and wrist watch as he was playing football that afternoon and he would collect them at dinnertime. Totally innocently I said I would, not thinking too much about it, but feeling slightly flattered to be asked, so of course I wasn't going to question it!

It didn't occur to me to wonder why he didn't leave them in his room, as his friend would have a key to let him in later. Maybe I didn't want it to occur to me.

Then at dinnertime, he arrived to collect his keys and watch. He stayed and chatted a little while, then he asked if he and his friend could hook up with my friends and me and would I save him a seat, or rather two, for him and his mate. Innocently I agreed to save two seats with our bunch of friends, feeling a little more flattered.

His Leading Lady

The keys and watch and saving seats interest continued all week. He invited me to watch him play football one day, which I did, even though I'm not a fan. The penny was beginning to drop, that there was quite possibly going to be a romance, but I was really enjoying the rush of being pursued.

Three or four days into the festival my friend pointed out to me that she thought he 'liked' me!

Well, in that moment I was given all the confirmation I needed. Though it had crossed my mind, I had ignored it as unlikely, but in that instant I could see it and feel it. I became completely love sick; I went off my food, I couldn't sleep, the excitement was overwhelming.

I was falling in love, being swept off my feet and I couldn't wait for the next day. I was used to being flirted with, so the keys and watch thing and the saving of seats wasn't really enough to mean anything more than flirtatious. I now believed it was meaning something more, that I was being wooed, chased and romanced and I was more than flattered. I was falling head over heels in love with this lovely, handsome man!

The next day I was more than excited for what it held. At the end of the evening after we had supper in someone else's room, we all walked back to my room, him and me, his friend and my friends. However, because I was now aware of his possible intentions, I needed to do some checking out of my own, so I drew back from the crowd, to see if he would linger with me. He did, noticeably obviously, so I slipped my arm through his and he seemed happy with this by giving my arm a gentle squeeze.

When we reached my room I got a very appropriate peck on the cheek! We were on the same page, he does like me and I do like him, very much!

With a smile on my face and a skip in my step, my heart beating a little faster, I joined my friends who were more than interested in all the details of our first romantic encounter.

49

The next day I met his parents, he met mine as both our families were at the festival. My parents loved him immediately.

That evening we went out for our first date. We borrowed his father's car. We drove to the nearest beach. We walked, held hands and talked. He bought a bag of chips from the chip shop. We continued walking as we shared the chips. Had I really found the love of my life? I hoped so. Years later his mother told me that when she first met me she felt I was sincere.

I was – most definitely sincere. I knew that if her son had fallen in love with me, and asked me to marry him I would be totally devoted to him for the rest of my life!

He waved me off as our coach drove away on the Saturday morning. He promised to phone me in a couple of days. Was this all too good to be true? Was it a dream? I prepared myself for the disappointment of finding out it was nothing more than a holiday romance and he would change his mind about me within a day or so.

He proved my insecurities wrong! Three weeks later he visited my home for a few days following speaking on the phone most evenings since we parted. Over these very few days together we grew in love so much more. We talked about marriage and family, we were both certain this was the beginning of a life-long commitment of marriage and children. More than one child, but no more than three was our joint agreement.

We swapped stories about our childhoods. His stories were far more interesting than mine. I learned early in our relationship that his parents had adopted him, he had known since he was nine years old.

They told him of being specially chosen by them and how much they loved him and wanted him. He spoke fondly and proudly of his parents, he was very positive about his adoption.

We continued happily in a long distance relationship, apart from occasional weekends together, until the summer. Distance definitely made my heart grow much fonder.

Time to reflect ...

Never underestimate the possibilities that are within you. When opportunity comes through a door of your life, embrace it and be prepared to be surprised with the outcomes. As a young woman I had so little self-belief that I would shake my head and retreat in fear of incompetence and failure at the opportunity to venture into the unknown. Because of this I made a promise to God and myself that whatever opportunity or invitation presented itself, I would say *YES!* I became an *'I Can Do'* person instead of an *'I Cannot Do'* person. One of the best choices I made...

Pray...

Heavenly Father, take my life now and begin to reveal your purposes through me.

Show me where to invest and what to walk away from. Show me what to embrace and what to let go. Help me to discover my talents and gifts and lead me into opportunities to learn new skills that will enhance your will and design for my future.

Amen

Proverbs 3:5

Trust God from the bottom of your heart; don't try to figure out everything on your own.
Listen for God's voice in everything you do, everywhere you go; He's the one who will keep you on track.

(The Message)

Two Became One – Then There Were Three

Hang my locket around your neck,
wear my ring on your finger.
Love is invincible facing danger and death.
Passion laughs at the terrors of hell.
The fire of love stops at nothing,
It sweeps everything before it.
Flood waters can't drown love,
Torrents of rain can't put it out.
Love can't be bought, love can't be sold.

Song of Solomon 8:6-8 (The Message)

There was no doubt in my mind that he was the one I would spend the rest of my life with. We were compatible in many ways, but opposite when it came to football, rugby, cricket, sewing, knitting and crochet.

His family were Christians; we had been raised with identical beliefs, morals and values. Now our pursued desire to study theology brought our lives together. Following our studies, Handsome would apply for the ministry – and so become a Reverend, there was little doubt that he would be accepted within the organisation we belonged to.

During August that year we spent a whole two weeks together in Northern Ireland, the country of his birth. We had planned to get engaged during this holiday.

Reverend Grey

The journey to Northern Ireland was an example of events we were to become familiar with, being the first of many of our 'skin of the teeth' experiences.

On the way to Stranraer to catch the ferry, I took over the driving somewhere north of the Lake District on the M6. He fell fast asleep as I drove on past the junction we were supposed to leave the motorway at, not realising until he woke up. We took the next exit, having gone miles out of our way. We needed petrol, but if we wandered around looking for a filling station we would miss the ferry.

We continued in the direction of Stranraer and hoped there were services on the way. Should we drive fast enough to get there on time, which meant using more petrol? But if we drove slowly we would be late! We took the risk to get there on time and hope to pass a filling station. There was no fuel station, or services and the light on the dashboard was on for many miles to signal the need for petrol. We got to the ferry in the nick of time.

We had travelled about ninety miles with the fuel gauge showing empty. Unbelievably, when it was time to drive off the ferry at Larne the engine started without a spit or splutter. Within a few minutes we sighed with relief to see a filling station!

At the first opportunity we became engaged. We headed off to do some shopping in Belfast city; it was the summer of 1981. My fiancé was in a changing room trying on a pair of trousers when, with a rush of sudden intensity, shoppers began hastily completing their purchases.

I told him it had thundered and everyone was hurrying to get their shopping done. That's not thunder, it's a bomb he replied!

We were in Northern Ireland at the time of 'The Troubles', but I had not anticipated bombs! My fiancé was already dressed and we left the department store. Roads were closed off, smoke filled the streets, and police and army were out in force to direct the public to safety.

Two Became One – Then There Were Three

I already felt safe. I had just got engaged to my superhero who knew exactly where to go to get us out of the panic. He did take us through the Falls Road, a very dangerous place for a car with an English number plate in 1981 and he got a sharp telling off from his mother for driving through that road.

What an amazing summer we had. I was incredibly happy! I felt like the princess who got her prince! A fairy tale bride to be! I had done well.

> *The rose coloured spectacles made me blind to how indefensible I was to becoming the victim of his predetermined bias.*

After many full and fun days we were on our way home. We caught a very late ferry to save money. It was about 3am when we debarked in Stranraer. We motored for an hour or so on dark country lanes, by which time we needed to sleep for at least an hour. We came to a lay-by, the ones that are totally off the road, behind a verge of trees and a grass boarder and can be entered and exited from both ends.

My fiancé drove into the lay-by, stopped, turned off the engine. We were both asleep within seconds. Unknowingly to each other, while it was still very dark, we both opened our eyes to see an articulated lorry approaching us. The driver had entered the lay-by from the opposite end and he was heading straight for us.

My fiancé flashed his headlights in time for the lorry driver to steer himself around us! We closed our eyes and fell back to sleep, we didn't so much as look at one another, or say anything to each other either! Hours later when we were continuing our journey home, I remembered the lorry in the middle of the night. We both recounted the same moment in exactly the same detail! I would have thought it a dream had he not described the precise account of what I had remembered.

We arranged for our wedding to take place during the Easter holidays of the following year. I was excited, I couldn't wait to be his wife.

For the next few months while planning our wedding we spent every bit of time we could together, getting to know each other and things we agreed on and there were of course things we disagreed on. As far as the wedding plans were concerned, we agreed on everything.

My naïve expectation was that we would enjoy a long, happy and exciting marriage. Any troubles and challenges we faced would be insignificant compared with our happiness. It would be his primary responsibility to make sure his future family were provided for and protected. It was my responsibility alongside part time jobs when necessary, to make a home that would create an environment for refuge, nurture, love and comfort. This was the 1980s and I was more than delighted to be the primary homemaker.

Our combined weaknesses and flaws were already set up to fail each other, as I had the gullible vulnerability that would provide the ever expanding allowances for the wilful indiscretions my loved one needed to satisfy his troubled mind.

> *We were a perfect storm! I needed him, he needed a secret keeper!*

As I look back I remember that nothing was too much for him to do for me. He 'pandered' to my every whim. Of course I wasn't intentionally expecting this of him. What I interpreted as him being purely romantic was combined with his want to please and possibly earn my love as a probable result of the neglect he suffered as an infant. He didn't believe he had a choice, his default was set to give me every pleasure he could, to please me in every way possible, making him the answer to the surfacing of my insecurities, to compensate for them, to step in when I wavered, or felt overwhelmed.

Subtly, it was the unseen child in him that perpetuated my dependencies. It must have been tiresome, the constant pressure to please. Neither of us recognised the precedent we were setting. The wheels buckled under the pressure occasionally, without realisation we were navigating our own ruin. Never imagining one day the tandem would completely fall apart.

> *The need of the child in me was met with the needs of the child in him.*

We had a lovely wedding day, one week before Easter. I loved being a bride, anticipating being my bridegroom's bride for life. I had made up my mind to enjoy every moment, as there wouldn't be another wedding day for me. It was a simple but meaningful wedding, it was the best day of my life so far, and I wanted to remember how wonderful it felt marrying the love of my life.

We flew to Spain the following day, the weather was very hot and neither of us had been abroad before. We couldn't wait to get on the beach, swim in the sea and enjoy the sun and each other.

We went to a local restaurant for a full English breakfast. My new husband was very keen to have his first attempt at making sure the waitress understood his order of two English breakfasts and two mugs of tea. He gesticulated expressively, using his very limited Spanish along with pointing to the menu. It was a bit of a pantomime really, the waitress stood there patiently watching and listening to him slowly and loudly finish our order, while writing in her note pad. My husband finished his party piece, looking at the waitress, smiling as she responded, "That'll be two English breakfasts and two mugs of tea," in a very thick Liverpudlian accent! We giggled like a couple of kids.

We enjoyed evenings as we strolled and ate waffles running with warm chocolate sauce.

The honeymoon was over; we were in our first home together.

I had lay in on this our first morning of the rest of our lives. This was to be the first of hundreds and thousands of mugs of tea in bed for me to wake up to. My husband, it appeared, was an early bird. Not me. That is why I woke up to a cup of tea made for me every morning for most of our marriage. While sitting up in bed drinking my tea, I could hear a noise. He was hoovering! In the 80s, every vacuum cleaner was called a Hoover. I wanted to be the first to use our brand new hoover, I wanted to play house.

I cannot explain how I have managed to survive the double life of Reverend *Grey* that we sustained for over thirty years. I can only invite you into our story at the very beginning of our marriage and describe the backdrop; the backstage, wings and props behind every scene and what unfolded behind the public presentation of our *'Perfect Life'*.

I was in character, dressed for the role I was born for and knew I would love. There were no rehearsals, we were given no lines to learn and neither of us had any experience of the expectations that lay before us.

There was only going to be one take of the 'Drama' of our life:

Lights – Camera – Action. We're on!
It's the opening scene of the very real life presentation called
'Reverend Grey'.
I assumed my character – I did my best for the audience of
Mr and Mrs Public.

Time to reflect …

Maybe you are in a situation where some or all of your hopes, dreams and expectations have short changed you.

Your life reflects very little of what was promised.

Perhaps you feel hopeless and dreamless, you are lost in circumstances outside of your control and there appears no possibility of things changing for the better.

Whether the disappointments are a result of intentional recklessness like mine or not, you are suffering and there is no easy or swift way for change, short of a miracle.

Pray with me...

Heavenly Father, I give you all my disappointment, disillusionment and hopelessness.

I am tired and worn out of feeling lost and alone in my dissatisfactions. I am exhausted with putting on my happy face, pretending that everything is fine.

I confess now of anything I have done to add to my situation (name those things that you know have been wrong).

Forgive me, Father, and help me to do what is right in place of the wrongs I have done.

I call upon your Great Name to help me, to renew hope and trust that my circumstances can change and show me what I can do to help others and myself.

Amen

Jeremiah 29:11

This is God's Word on the subject: "I'll show up and take care of you as I promised and bring you back home. I know what I'm doing. I have it all planned out – plans to take care of you, not abandon you, plans to give you the future you hope for".

(The Message)

Reverend Grey

Part 2

Scene 1
Fatal Perceptions

I miss – when he tells me I am beautiful, that my skin is so soft.
The ping on my phone is his text to say "on my way home".

He took care of everything. I was secure in his competence to know what to do in every situation we faced. He was only three years older than me; it felt more like ten. I put him on a pedestal. I could see no wrongs in him. He always put my happiness before his own, saying if I was happy, then he was too.

My world grew larger when I married my husband. My children and I are blessed and have benefitted enormously from the relational associations and friends we have, because of who my husband is, for which I am very grateful.

We were only married for a matter of weeks, I had gone into the bedroom for something. One of my absolutely greatest fears was larger than life on the bedroom floor. I let out this blood curdling, ear piercing scream, as I was desperate to alert my new super hero to rescue me from the biggest, blackest, ugliest, furriest, eight legged spider I had ever seen! I should have warned him about my intense repulsion at the sight of these creatures, as I did not expect him to come running into the room faster than the speed of light with a posture posed to fight off an axe murderer! All bright red, eyes bulging, and his biceps bursting like Popeye having just eaten spinach!

Reverend Grey

There was an advertisement popular on TV when we were first married, it was for the Prudential. The line that kept repeating through the advert was different people saying, "I wanna be..." The final actor's line was "I wanna be together" spoken with a Midland English accent and the expression of an annoying overgrown wimp! The Reverend used to say that was my line as I liked us to do things together. He didn't mean that as a compliment though. He was making fun of me, twisting the emphasis on me wanting us to do every together in some clingy annoying way!

I wonder now as I contemplate, was his subconscious opinion of me paralleled to an annoying overgrown wimp? If so, I may have deserved it – the child in me needed the assurance I was sharing my life with someone, being one part of a whole.

My mind-set had switched from being single to being a couple almost immediately, unlike his. He would talk about things regarding both of us in the context of I, me and mine instead of we, us and ours. I often sensed, in my quiet moments, that there was a very small part of the Reverend that was holding something back from me. I paid it no attention, as joining together in marriage was a unique transition for everyone.

I would make a point of correcting him when he should have said ours, but instead said mine. He would follow that up by quoting "I wanna be together" in the sad wimpish voice as acted on TV.

It is my perception that the Reverend grew accustomed to making fun of me. I was fine and laughed along when we were alone, or with family because his quick wit was very funny.

I became the butt of jokes when we were in company or he was public speaking, which became quite common especially at weddings. Eventually I asked him to stop as it was increasingly upsetting me as I learned over the years how badly his disloyalties were. He was making too many public withdrawals that were pulling on my emotional and mental health, without depositing the credits for him to withdraw from.

I still struggle to cope with being made fun of, being the butt of condescending jokes that demean. I'm not referring to the times I do something silly, they are many and I'm the first to laugh at myself.

The biggest entity I brought into our marriage was my great need of him, my knight in shining armour, and the answer to all my cares. I would never have to walk alone in the dark ever again. He would look after me every day for the rest of our lives.

> *I knew I would be a great wife. I loved my husband and wanted to please him. I was domesticated so I could run a home well, then eventually would be a good mother to our children.*

The vast skill mix and qualifications I have acquired over more than thirty years was, to a large degree, attributed to the belief my husband had in me. He allowed me time to learn at my own pace and to excel in my strengths in the areas I was passionate about. I was one of life's late developers.

I am who I am now, and I like who I am now, I wouldn't trade my life for anybody's, all because of my marriage, my family and our many varied experiences, roles and functions.

My husband's application to enter the Christian ministry was accepted and he became a 'Reverend'. In the mean time we were expecting our first child. I could not wait to be a mummy, and I knew it would be my greatest joy.

In the very early stages of pregnancy we went on holiday in our much-loved Morris Traveller which we had bought from the Reverend's family. Excitedly, we motored through the English countryside. A motorcyclist came round a bend at high speed and clipped our driver's side back wing, ripping off the wooden trim from along the side of the body.

The Reverend stopped in the middle of the road, leapt out of the car leaving the door wide open and took off running and flapping his arms after the cyclist who didn't stop to take responsibility for his careless driving. The Reverend was hopping mad as I fell about laughing at him running after a motorbike.

Again that same summer, further into pregnancy, in our marvellous 'moggy', we set off to have a look around the seaside town that would be our next home. We didn't have much money, it was too far to go in one day so we flattened the rear seats in the car, zipped two sleeping bags together, took the pillows from our bed, packed a soap bag each, and slept overnight in the back of the moggy.

We spent the night in the overnight car park at a motorway services. Just as well it was summer! We didn't bother with a change of clothes; we washed our faces and cleaned our teeth in the Ladies and Gents, then set off for the rest of our adventure. We couldn't tell anyone because it was top secret! I don't think we have ever told anybody about this exciting secret mission, it was one of our good secrets. A warm and wonderful memory.

Several months ahead, still totally smitten with the Reverend I went into labour a few days after my due date. We were so happy to welcome our first-born joy into our lives. The Reverend was a brilliant father from the start.

By this time we were living with our little baby in an upstairs bedroom/sitting room flat that someone kindly allowed us to use. It was an interim place while waiting for our first position to materialise. I had mild postnatal blues.

One day I remember being incredibly moody. The Reverend was on his way out of the flat, I didn't want him to leave and he didn't have to go out, but he went to leave anyway. I was so mad with him! As he was walking down the stairs I took an item of clothing I was drying on the banister at the time and threw it at him, followed by the others! I couldn't yell because the lady of the house was downstairs.

He still went out, he had too. Then I had to go and pick up the clothes and place them back on the banister to dry. We were both quite stubborn and defiant with our own set of ideals when we were first married.

Considering wedded bliss, it can take years to mould together to become bonded as a couple. When you are, it is precious to have that one person in the world that complements you, and both can appreciate each other's differences. Then embrace and accept them and with patience and love make them work for the advantage of your marriage and family life. It is well worth all the conflict it takes to get there.

Our first child was only five weeks old when we were introduced to our first congregation. It was both exciting and daunting, though we knew we were born for this role, my husband was a natural as a Reverend.

We moved into our third home, for the first time as a family of three.

We were happily married, but there were the obvious challenges. We were a young couple, newly married with a new baby, in a new home, in a new town, amongst new people, fulfilling roles we were both new to.

We didn't have any family members close by, we were gradually settling down, and only had our congregation to make friends with, and find those who we could rely on for support. There were some lovely friendships made.

Things were as good as they could be, we had the normal hitches of a new couple, learning to live with each other but in the main we were very happy and compatible.

I admit though, as a young wife, I could begin an argument about which way the wind blew! I could occasionally exhibit a short fuse and wouldn't be very tolerant if things didn't go my way, as I genuinely thought I knew best.

The problem was that the Reverend genuinely thought he knew best too. We were two firebrands so sparks were often flying.

I could be relentless in conflict!

At the point of a frustration that had nowhere else to go, the Reverend would leave the house.

I totally understood why he would leave, in normal situations it was a good thing to do – to put space between us until reason and rationale resumed so that harmony and affection could be restored. Thankfully neither of us tended to store up resentment, we were not a couple for feuds!

Over the years intuition provoked perceptions which messed with my mind. Then, when the Reverend left the house after an argument it caused me even more worry, more anger and hostility towards him, as I couldn't trust him not to do something foolish, he found disloyalties easier if he was angry with me and me him.

After a year of living in the lovely holiday town we had a toddler and another baby on the way. While being very excited to be making another baby, my worries began. He would often be late home, and then it began to happen more regularly. I would be pacing the kitchen floor, waiting for his car to pull up on the driveway, well past midnight sometimes. I had no way of contacting him to put my mind at ease about where he was.

There was always a reasonable explanation; he was kept behind talking, he lost his way or the car broke down, there was an accident or he fell asleep when he parked up to take a break because he was tired!

I had no way to prove anything other than what he had said, I had no choice but to accept his word and believe him. The alternative, that he was lying, to cover up an awful truth was unthinkable at the time.

Already I was picking up on behaviours that signalled all was not as it should be. I was losing confidence in his reliability, which was very sad. I knew married life was not easy and the perfect man or woman doesn't exist. I was troubled and felt uneasy for some undisclosed reason regarding my husband.

> *I have learned that it takes years to build up trust. All it takes is suspicion to destroy it.*

So what if the Reverend hadn't been completely straight with me? Maybe I set too high expectations on him, and judged him unfairly when he didn't arrive home on time. How many of us would choose to make a good excuse rather than find ourselves in conflict?

The benefit of the doubt was the only way I could move on from my disquiet, as it was only suspicion. What I was actually suspicious of I had no idea at the time.

Time to reflect ...

If this chapter has sparked some recognition in your life and relationships say this prayer with me.

Heavenly Father, I place into your hands all the misgivings and perceptions that I carry, my lack of confidence and self-worth that cause co-dependencies and the need for constant affirmation and reassurance.

Enable me to grow in a sense of acceptance for who I am and not in skills and abilities. Help me to believe in myself to attain and gain everything I am destined for regardless of any failures and setbacks that have hindered my way forward in the past.

I look to you for help where others have promised and not kept their word, I trust you to be faithful to all you have promised.

Amen

Psalm 46:1

God is a safe place to hide; ready to help when we need him.

(The Message)

Scene 2

The Unwelcome Guest

I miss – The sound of his key in the door,
The love of my life walking mud on the floor,
The leap inside at the sound of his voice,
His company of familiar noise.

We moved house the following spring, still in the same seaside town. I was six months pregnant and getting quite a big baby bump. This would be our fourth home and soon to be a family of four.

I went into the early stages of labour on my due date and our daughter was born; again we were overwhelmed with our bundle of joy on her arrival.

I was thrilled to arrive home being a family of four, having no idea how my two children were going to contend with each other from a very early age.

We had two strong characters in the making. Shaping their strengths without killing them in the process would be a challenge, but for now, a tiny baby girl and a very caring big brother was just wonderful.

We would often invite friends for the evening, young children made it more difficult to go out, having friends over was something we could do to broaden our social network.

Reverend Grey

A couple were coming for dinner, they were arriving at seven. I had prepared the meal, fed, bathed and put our two babies down for the night, tidied the house laid the table.

Everything was ready to greet our guests just before they arrived. There was only one problem – the Reverend wasn't home! This was stressful enough for me, when I was in my twenties, to put on a dinner party for guests who I didn't know very well, it only added to the stress that their host wasn't home.

He arrived at the same time as them, apologising for being late, explaining that he had fallen asleep on the beach, which amused everyone. I complied with the majority and laughed along with our guests, but worry silently nagged again.

> *Suspicion increased and poison pervaded the dark aura like an unexpected damp chill that blows through the night.*

Later that year we were offered another ministerial position. The Reverend went for an interview. The situation felt right for us so we accepted the transfer to a much larger city church. It was a great congregation, lots of families, young mums and people we would remain in touch with all our lives. We moved to our fifth home, which was very temporary while we house hunted for a more permanent home, plus we were able to arrange our first mortgage together.

We drove away from a beautiful seaside town with wonderful coastline, beaches and scenery, to arrive a couple of days later in a jam packed city of bumper to bumper buses, taxis and cars and high rise buildings. Graffiti covered almost every public wall; broken glass lay in pieces around every bus shelter. Homeless people slept in doorways, parkways and tunnels.

It felt like home immediately – which confirmed this was where we were meant to be for sure.

The Unwelcome Guest

The very first Sunday morning we had a terrible argument arriving for the service both very frustrated with each other. We had only moved there three days earlier, with two little ones who were unsettled and had slept very little, we were probably very stressed. We parked the car and wondered why it was so quiet, no one to be seen. Then it dawned on us the clocks had gone back an hour through the night meaning we were an hour early. Relieved, we were able to go home, have a cuppa, sort our attitudes out then start the day again.

We fell into the groove of city life; we loved the buzz and busyness of our new setting.

Months passed as we quickly made ourselves at home. We were among many wonderful people, living in our sixth home as we got our first mortgage. Life was good, plans were coming together, we were very happy and in a good position for success.

It didn't take more than a few months of living in this city before uncertainty regarding the Reverend began to ring its unwelcome bells. I recognised those bell ringers called fear, doubt and suspicion.

Within the first year, I had called the police twice, possibly three times because he hadn't arrived home and it was long past midnight. I was panic stricken, expecting him home by ten thirty at the latest.

Drug and alcohol addiction was prevalent, along with prostitution, domestic violence and abuse. Knife crime was rampant. Aids and HIV had recently begun claiming its victims. This city was rife with all these addictions and diseases as well as Hepatitis B and C. During this time many casualties presented themselves, not only among our church community, but we came face to face with vulnerable and dangerous situations on our doorstep too. The Reverend would not hesitate to get involved in potentially hostile circumstances if it meant he could help or rescue one precious person.

Reverend Grey

The first time I met a self-harmer she arrived unannounced on our doorstep for help. She showed me her one-inch wide, six-inch long scars along her inner thighs. This lovely teenage child had viewed herself so worthless she had slashed her own thighs to ribbons to mask her greater pain of violent abuse. When the Reverend did arrive home, police were in our living room, he gave his reasons for being so late, and he was believable.

Typically I soon forgot about these infrequencies, writing them off as the mysteries of men who can lose all sense of time when out and about at work. This is particularly the case with the work of a Reverend, as there is always another task that needs attention, a person to visit or a meeting that runs over time.

However, I clearly remember being in bed one night. Our two children were very young and fast asleep. Suddenly I was awake, feeling alarmed. I was aware of an unwelcome presence in our bedroom. Naturally it was dark as it was the middle of the night, but the dark presence I detected was tangible as if someone evil and menacing was in the room. I woke my husband and told him what I was feeling. I used the language we would be familiar with, saying, "I think there is an evil spirit in our room", and I asked him to deal with it. He did and the evil left the bedroom, as it should, because when Jesus said we would drive out demons in His Name, we believed it to be true, *(Matthew 10:1).*

Casting my mind back to this experience now, I cannot help but wonder, had my husband through his curiosity in pornography opened himself up to an unholy spirit? I sincerely believe evil left when the Reverend prayed. Did the Reverend open himself up to evil again through an even deeper involvement in pornography? The Reverend definitely did that not too long after this alarming and unexpected experience.

I cannot remember why I would look under the driving seat floor mat in the car, I cannot recall what reason sent me looking for what I did not want to find. Maybe it was that same dark

Time to reflect ...

Are you living with uncertainty in your life at the moment? Do you feel uncomfortable but don't know why?

If you find yourself indulging in fantasies of a sexual nature and have a growing desire to make them real by acting them out, maybe you are on a slippery slope where you know you could spiral out of control one day. If you are harbouring bad secrets, either your own or someone else's, they will close in on you one day and force themselves into the open. Or perhaps you have made an unholy agreement with someone and are trapped in his or her lie. You need to find someone to talk to. The risk might be high, like mine was, and you may feel you cannot face the outcome of your disclosure. The risk is far higher the longer you keep quiet.

Let me pray for you;

Heavenly Father, I pray for the person reading this prayer now that you will allay their fears and give them the confidence to speak to someone about their concerns.

They were not created to carry worries and anxieties, for now we hand them over to you. In prayer I lift all the worries off their heart and mind and place them in your care.

You know exactly what the perfect plan is to set him or her free; you know who the best person for them to confide in is.

Bring this person into their path soon and show them a clear sign to confirm to them who this is.

If these are the hidden secrets of this person, I pray for the people who are possibly being affected in some negative way, I pray you will protect relationships and friendships and guide all concerned into peace and freedom.

Should the secrets be the doing of another and an unreliable soul tie has been forged, I pray for wisdom that will know exactly what they should do in their unique and personal circumstances.

Amen

Psalm 118:5-16

Pushed to the wall, I called to God; from the wide open spaces, he answered.
God's now at my side and I'm not afraid...

(The Message)

Scene 3

Don't Mind Me – I Won't Tell

I miss – the smile in his eyes as he sees my face,
The silly big wave that makes me giggle,
As the man in the middle,
Feels out of place.

I was not a deterrent, who could stop the Grey One if I didn't? Sadly he continued in his growing addiction.

There was now a life beneath the surface, a basement room to our marriage that no one must see. There were no windows, only the trap door that was covered by a rug with a thick, twisted pile of secrets. Cloned in an image of intimacy, we were emotionally shackled to a course of actions that were steered by the Grey One's perversions.

> *Everything the Grey One did, everything I found, went into the 'Cellar of Secrets', padlocked with an unspoken agreement of silence.*

The Grey One is charming, but charm comes in many disguises. It can be turned on at will to attract likability.

The Grey One had been out of my sight for a while, but he was never too far away, skulking in the shadows. For a while, however, I forgot about the magazines and that awful letter.

Sometime later we were away for a weekend, visiting friends. Our two toddlers were with us. I discovered something else, something I hadn't expected. His other self, the Grey One, became personified. The dark shadow of the Reverend's invisible challenger literally crawled into my light of day.

He admitted nothing and denied everything; this became his insistent and constant defence. He had no choice, it was his way of trying to protect me, but sadly it was never going to do that.

The unearthing of dark behaviour being quite rare in our early years, it was still very disturbing when discoveries were made. After a day or so my naïveté and lack of experience dulled the fears I wasn't ready to acknowledge. I chose to pop it in the basement as another mystery.

The Grey One was in our marriage to stay and would become more needy of the Reverend's thoughts, time and practice.

Charm cannot be trusted as a characteristic of substance.

His grim determination relentlessly chiselled away with persistence at the Reverend's weak will, with the planned goal of attaining number one position between the two personalities. His plan from the start was to displace the identity of the Reverend, by removing everything and everyone out of his life that made him who he was.

Then baby number three was on the way sooner than we had planned. We were very happy, we wanted three children, we were affording our lifestyle, there was no reason to be anything other than overjoyed.

One month before baby's due date, impeccable timing on our part, the Reverend decided to take a few days off to redesign our back garden making it more convenient for the children to play. This was destined to be a very interesting project. It was a big undertaking. Nothing, however, was too big a task for the unrestrained confidence the Reverend had in his ability to landscape our plot.

At eight and a half months pregnant I was holding up a cement mixer, with a bump about the same size, to prevent it from tipping over. I stood hugging this lump of metal while the Reverend took out some of the contents!

With great care he continued to lay the concrete on the hard core. Like most of our first attempts at DIY we learned what not to do next time. The Reverend had cemented himself in at the far corner of our new patio! Without going into unnecessary details the only way to get back to the front of the garden was across the wet cement.

Not only did the Reverend have to negotiate his leap over the wet, freshly laid concrete, he had to do so carrying a large bag of sand – unless he was prepared to stand there until it dried.

Within a few days bundle of joy number three came along. As with his brother and sister we were delighted at the arrival of our second baby boy, he completed our family.

The Reverend was an engaging father who adored his family and always went above and beyond to help them achieve their best. He was their hero who they looked up to with love and respect, they were proud to be his kids.

He willingly put himself out for us all without a second thought.

On the scale of one to ten he was up there at the top, as a father and a husband. He allowed the children to express their opinions, he freed them to have a voice among our friends and colleagues which gave them a confidence to hold their own in communicating within a variety of social settings, helping them to a maturity beyond their years.

I struggled to stay afloat due to the Grey One's growing troubles which impacted on my emotional and mental health quite severely.

There were times I could not be who my children needed me to be, but they were very much wanted and very much loved and cared for and earnestly prayed for.

There are only so many times you can have the stuffing knocked out of you before you find yourself with little reserve. I ran on a very small amount of emotional fuel.

By this time we had been married for five years and apart from the first few months I was either pre-natal, post-natal or pre-menstrual. I was emotional even without the Grey One to add to my anxieties. I felt as though I spent the first seven years of marriage crying – I cried a lot, I mean a lot. I wasn't miserable, most times I was happy and would laugh a lot too. The Reverend would make me smile even through my tears. It is quite legitimate for women to cry for no reason, this is just the way it is with some of us from the age of about eleven! I had many reasons to weep as well as all the no reason, reasons!

Money became very tight due to rising interest rates on our mortgage. We had bought into the 1980s schemes of buy now, pay later, so we had debts to pay off. I was quite emotionally fragile, probably mildly depressed. On would go "the perfect life" appearance, when required, but in private, life was very difficult, although it was probably no more challenging than it was for many who were in our situation, and I was probably far better off than most.

There was always an exciting edge to life, lots to anticipate and look forward to. When belonging to an organisation as we were, life often took an unexpected turn for the better, with a constant opportunity for spontaneity, enjoyment and celebration.

The Reverend and I carried a strong disposition to make the best of every situation and see beyond the strife, from whatever direction it came.

We were a good strong team, we stood firmly together, always positive about the future. As easily as things often turned for the worse, there were numerous times when things turned for the better.

When I refer to life being hard, I am referring to the added anxieties of the unexpected blows from the Grey One's personal and private exposures. Alongside what I recognise now as more than likely suffering from clinical depression.

One thing was for sure in my mind, I believed in us that we would survive the worst and rise above all our squabbles, differences and challenges, to conquer the world and never give up on each other.

Time to reflect …

In public, with friends, while working, I appeared happy and smiling. I would engage with people confidently who sought me out for advice, help or support. I don't think I was ever moody or sulky in front of anyone other than my husband.

At home was different, I was very low and demotivated at times. I threw myself into bringing up the children, caring for them. The family did keep me busy, but there was continual underlying unrest.

When I could I put the worries out of my mind and got on with life, ignoring the constant chisel at my skull.

If this is you don't ignore it, your mental health is too important. I didn't understand this at the time. You may think you're okay, but you're not okay really. The only way to put yourself right is to do something about yourself. Mental health professionals are far more aware of matters of the mind and emotions than they were thirty years ago.

If I had known then what I know now, I would have at least made an appointment with my GP. I advise you to do the same, as well as finding a confidential ear.

Let's pray…

Father, I pray you will protect the heart mind and emotions from further damage and you will bring clarity to the fore that will make sense of everything confusing and that there will be action taken in place of apathy and false hope.

Amen

John 14:27

That's my gift to you. Peace.

I don't leave you the way you're used to being left – feeling abandoned, bereft.

So don't be upset. Don't be distraught.

(The Message)

Scene 4

miPhone – Innovation Liberated

He makes a good cup of tea,
My husband a unique brand,
My right hand.

Suspicion causes a most torturous anguish. Then to turn it on its head to accuse me of paranoia and an overactive imagination in an attempt to allay my suspicions and cause me to question myself – this created even more anxiety as it cast doubt on the stability of my mind. Yes, the Reverend really did create chaos in my head.

All his love and kindness was compromised by the continued foolishness of the Grey One, I hoped I would see the last of him one day.

More than that, I became the keeper of more and more secrets that lay underneath the rug that they all got swept underneath.

Reverend Grey risked my health and was extremely blind to the consequences of his addiction!

As time went on it wasn't necessary to use Royal Mail for pornography and prostitution anymore because another, far darker opportunity came on the market to keep secrets and enable deceit.

A huge brick of a contraption called a car phone was given to the Reverend. Only he used it, and now along with me, it would keep his secrets.

It wasn't long before he was getting cryptic phone calls, but of course I had no way of checking or verifying them.

I would ask questions, but the grey area served its purpose for the Grey One's benefit. He would tell me he had appointments to see people. I wouldn't know who they were. It would be late at night sometimes when he was supposedly called to an emergency. Emergencies did happen, but I was too intuitive and suspicious for my own good. What could I do? I had no leads to verify or disclaim his word, but all I knew was I didn't and couldn't trust him.

This was a very dark time because the Grey One's deeds were completely invisible, I had no idea what might be going on in his secret, private life. He didn't need to write letters or keep magazines. Contact details could be all stored in his cell phone and I didn't have any access to it.

I spiralled into a deep depression, but not really recognising it. I knew nothing about the symptoms of depression, so I just soldiered on managing the home, the children and a part time job.

Because we were looking after a small congregation as we had recently relocated about 40 miles from the city, our services were voluntary, so the Reverend took on additional employment that meant he was away for two or three nights most weeks.

I was very suspicious of him while he was away, but I found no evidence or proof to confirm my concerns. He would be away, staying in hotels, a perfect opportunity for a growing addiction to find its fix. I had no way to find out the truth whether there were sexual encounters or not. Suspicion alone was scathing enough.

Then there came the Internet. I could not compete with this remarkable new technology and all the implications it had for us.

The Internet became my most dreaded adversary. I would lose my ground to it with increasing regulatory. The Internet made things far easier for the Grey One to feed his compulsive needs.

By now we were in home number nine and relocated to yet another town and congregation.

I was reduced to keeping my feet firmly on the rug that covered the trap door to the basement of betrayals.

I began to discover more and many inappropriate pictures, messages and emails, all with sexual content on our computer.

The age of technology brought worse revelations of pornographic interest. We would continue to argue, row and fight! I was tormented daily beyond my limits. I had no proof that revealed that he had gone beyond a computer screen to this date in our history. There was much evidence, but no actual proof.

All the pornography and Internet addiction and contacts with others was all undercover, never to be seen.

He knew I would keep his secrets, he knew I would not expose him. He knew I knew the stuff he got entangled in. Why could he not talk to me about it? What was his need to intentionally cause me such uncertainty and instability?

We continued the cycle of discovery, confrontation, arguing and then silence, and too soon came imminent forgiveness and reconciliation. This subtle practice was an art we were both good at. He would become quiet. I interpreted his silence as him being hurt because I didn't believe his lies. Alternatively, he was struggling desperately to protect me from the truth. There was no way he could tell the truth. He needed to get the Grey One back into the basement. Out of sight. It was like trying to get the Genie back in the bottle.

Reverend Grey

Of course, my role in Reverend Grey's duplicitous life was the sacrificial, selfless one. If I went off script to dominate the scene – strongly holding my ground, insisting on the truth – I would suffer the most, it would get me nowhere. For the sake of moving forward I would step back into the role I had written for myself.

I became depressed again for many months, at times I would be unable to see people, and I couldn't answer the door or the phone. Sometimes I just couldn't face a day.

The children would have gone to school, the Reverend and I finished breakfast, and at that point for many months I dreaded the next step, which was when he left the house for work, it was bursting the bubble of safety for me.

What websites would he view today? Who would he send messages to today? What plans would he make today? Trust was dangerously weak.

On one occasion on our way home from visiting friends a mobile phone was hurled out of the car window in anger as we travelled because a text message came up on the Reverend's screen, he got angry and defensive when I asked who it was. I pushed him to get an honest answer, an argument erupted and he threw the phone out of the window and asked me if I was satisfied!

Well, that only confirmed that he had someone to hide. I made the mistake of not accepting his word when a lie seemed so obvious. I pushed for an answer and I forced him to throw the phone away!

Of course I wasn't satisfied, but what was the point of continuing that line of enquiry? The Grey One was cornered and when cornered, I saw very directly that it didn't pay to forget my lines. He couldn't escape, so he threw the evidence away instead.

He needed to find a way to end the conflict without having to tell the truth. For that occasion the truth will never be found, because it lies among the undergrowth on the side of a dual carriageway between two cities.

Another of his phones I threw out of our bedroom window into the bushes beyond our short garden. Nothing I did, however, made any difference. The worst was still going to come.

There was a woman called Sally, this is what the Grey One called her. Her message came into the Reverend's mobile phone one evening while he was out. He had forgotten to take his phone with him; I answered her texts as though I was him.

I discovered an email trail where it was evident the Grey One had met a women called Noreen, her on-line name, in a city over one hundred miles from where we were living. They had met on two occasions, when I believed my husband was working away for two or three days.

I had no proof if adultery had been committed, and no proof that it hadn't! Denial was always his defence.

Unusually for us, this upset lasted for days. The pressure was mounting as his fascinations grew. It was getting more difficult for him to cover up his secrets as they were piling up and I was expanding in my learning of computer technology.

The atmosphere grew so volatile between us. I didn't move on to the forgiveness phase in the cycle. I arrived home from work one afternoon to discover a letter saying he was going away.

The drama was short lived as he came home the following evening.

Some close friends and colleagues and those in the position of overseeing the Reverend's spiritual and emotional well-being looked after us. They have all been extremely kind, supportive and generous in both their care and guardianship for us over many years. We were supported incredibly well, without anyone knowing the underlying facts. The Reverend was asked by one of his supervisors if he was struggling with secret sins, he denied he was.

With financial support we were able to plan an immediate holiday.

I was very pleased to have him home, and continue in his employment.

All was forgiven and the hope was that this close call of breaking up our marriage and family and losing his career would be enough to end his irrational impulses!

But no it wasn't. The Grey One grew more compelling in his influence and occupancy over Reverend Grey's lifestyle.

The Reverend lived on the edge of danger. He needed to step back from the edge, but that would not have been an option for him. He loved risk and I became used to that edge of dare in his fearless persona that captured so many others' hearts.

No one asked me if there was an underlying problem with my husband, following our mini breakdown. The reason was assumed and confirmed that we had financial difficulties, which was true. But that was not the problem the Reverend ran from.

With the utmost respect, men talking to men about men's private struggles, back in the eighties and nineties, was never going to lift the lid off our can of worms, especially when they were so deeply hidden and disguised by our strong bond of love, and more so our success.

Pornography is an unseen war that is growing underneath the surface of successful and respectable people, within their loving relationships.

The Internet is internationally valued and helpful in our developed world for educational, professional and social enterprise. If unwisely left to the discretion of children and young people without strong boundaries of its use and an understanding of the dangers, it will become a most devaluing and destructive tool.

Already online troubles are resulting in mental illness in young people, and in some cases, suicide. It will continue to wreak havoc on society in its most intimate form.

It will attack its victims in the very places of safety and security. In the bedroom, the classroom among family and friends.

Silently and slowly releasing its venom from the end of fingertips, with direct access to the mind. Vanquishing all pre warnings of danger, young adults are out to prove the world they know better than their overbearing parents and out dated educators.

In ten, fifteen years' time, today's young people will be our fathers and mothers, Politicians and spiritual Leaders, educational, welfare and health professionals who were never able to master their demons.

Following the afore mentioned near breakdown of our marriage the Reverend promised me he would never leave me again however bad things got.

I continued to keep Reverend Grey's secrets and bury the truth. I became blinded by his lies, giving myself to marriage, family and our vocation. I was careful to keep our lovely children in blissful ignorance of the truth behind the scenes of their parents' private life and we amazingly survived for many years.

There were long periods of calm between the chaos and in these times we enjoyed some very happy and meaningful moments and seasons.

We were privileged and blessed to host a season of spiritual renewal in church. As a congregation we were experiencing some wonderful miracles and life changing encounters.

But personally I was struggling more than ever with depression and longing to see the fog that hovered over me daily to disappear.

A couple that were also good friends were coming to speak to our congregation for a weekend of special meetings.

The thought of the Reverend leaving me would yield a sick, dark rush of panic and fear that would swell up from a place deep within me.

They had been experiencing a spiritual renewal in their church and personally too.

I was feeling very low by this time and was resigned to the fog.

During the first session, the talk given was about personal barrenness. It wasn't really relating to me until the speaker asked if anyone was feeling dry and unproductive to stand for prayer. In that moment I knew that was me, so I stood.

I was right on the front row under the speaker's nose. He and his wife, our friends, both came to pray for me.

As they did a feeling came over me. I felt God's presence as I had never felt Him before, I couldn't stand as I was overwhelmed by Holy Spirit. I fell on the floor and remained there for a very long time, knowing I was very different, that I was changed, in that moment. I felt genuine joy that has never left me from that day.

We enjoyed a very happy and fulfilling few years without the Other One. It had been a long time since any evidence of the Grey One, he was virtually forgotten – but he wasn't gone!

Time to reflect …

If anyone reading this is getting lost inside a painful and protective role for the person who should be equally loving you in return, don't give up – there may be time for you to gain your identity back and salvage a selfless relationship with equal expectations of each other. There is always someone to go to, someone who wants to equally protect you.

If you have children who spend too much time on the Internet, find a way to encourage them to do other things, ask for their help with tasks as a means to separate them from their phone or computer.

Arrange things to do as a family, or simply you and your child. If you notice they are struggling to withdraw from online activities it is time to talk to them to devise ways of weaning their computer time.

Pray…

Father God, grant wisdom to manage these difficulties and strength to put it into action for the welfare of minds and emotions.

Amen

2 Samuel 22:29

You, LORD, are my lamp; the LORD turns my darkness into light.

(The Message)

Reverend Grey

Scene 5

Kiss the Frog

The spell was cast, long to last...
He still breaths, waiting for heaven's touch.
It will only take a moment, to free Delilah's clutch.

We moved house again, in the same town, into home number ten.

The Reverend did leave me again. Following another argument about his morals. It was true to form, he had no alternative but to leave because he needed to find a way to take himself out of the conflict he had created.

When real evidence presented itself, I needed answers I was never going to get, so leaving would create an even bigger drama. This would subdue my anger against him, as him leaving was my greater fear. Once again, he unknowingly demonstrated to me the consequence of continuing in conflict with the Grey One. If I didn't want him to leave, I needed to let the Grey One go back into the shadows.

Honesty wasn't an option as the Grey One could not enter the light of day.

As awful as it all was, I don't believe he enjoyed causing so much division between us. He needed a coping strategy for his growing compulsive disorder.

Reverend Grey

The Reverend wasn't able to break free from the Grey One, so he needed a plan to reset the status.

There was no way he could explain the Grey One because he was an invisible fantasy and had to remain so. If I wasn't prepared to allow him to disappear, the Reverend had no option but to remove himself.

The Grey One, as I call him, became an integrated identity in the Reverend's life, separate from the rest of his identity and personality, and functioned entirely independently. The onus was always on me to adjust to his ever increasing obsessions.

It may not have been his intention but all this did was control and manipulate me into locking up my fears and keep up the pretence of 'the perfect life'. My only other option was to leave him, with my children. I could not and would not do that to the family or myself.

The Grey One had won as, from then on, I would concede to the Reverend who was also a victim to the unseen Grey one. I remained in character, as I did not want the Reverend to leave us.

I'm sure the Reverend didn't want to leave either, but rather he had to run away with the very uncomfortable Grey One when the Reverend could no longer wrestle with the scrutiny; he needed to get the Grey One out of the light.

The cycle continued and I kept on forgiving and apologising when the Grey One appeared back on stage.

It was a very emotional farewell when we moved from this town. We had such an amazing time with many wonderful experiences and fond memories that will never be forgotten. I made lifelong friends who I still love and appreciate very much.

We moved to another city, our eleventh home. Things were good for a while, as it was with every fresh start.

Whenever the Grey One's arousals resurfaced, to crave his longed for gratification and compulsion, the Reverend was powerless against him. The Grey One's needs had to be satisfied.

Following a period of abstinence from the addictions, the Grey One always returned stronger and more reckless than he had ever been previously! As expected it wasn't long before I recognised that 'he' was back in force!

I noticed the same person kept appearing in a text message on his phone. I didn't know her; she was around for quite a while. I had never before known a contact to continue for such a long time. She was not British; her written vocabulary was not good. As well as the inappropriate intimate nature of the messages, there was also general chatting, which brought a friendship aspect to the connections; this also I had not seen before.

As I stated earlier, whenever the Grey One came out of the basement to arrest the mind of the Reverend after a period of absence, his capacity for deeper and darker betrayals grew.

I messaged the woman, to let her know who she was in contact with. I then decided to buy a cheap mobile phone and contact him anonymously as a person he would have met on line.

When I did the response I received back was shocking. He wanted me, to please me. He told me his preference was to give pleasure. He was desperate to meet me, without ever verifying who I was.

Those explorations lasted weeks so that I would know what extreme lengths he would go to.

He had no idea that while he was at the dining table working, without him noticing I would text him as this anonymous person. I would be sat only yards away from him.

He would always respond quickly and inappropriately.

Personal grooming began to take on new habits.

The thought of being the one to change our lives forever was not one to consider.

Denials only appeared to be letting him off now. Denials, as the Reverend's defence, became obvious lies. The excuses and cover stories were not making sense – they were irrational.

Though choosing to believe him was ludicrous, it also took away his need to look at his own foolishness.

But I was far from stupid! He knew it, but he couldn't afford to allow himself to tell the truth.

I understood what the Grey One expected from me, in the portrayal of my role in the drama called 'our marriage'. However, I was still likely to veer out of character when provoked beyond my ability to remain true to cast.

> *Subtly and slowly I was distorting into acceptance, but not approval, towards the Grey One.*

Occasionally I would search the car, just to see what I could find. These searches whether it was the car, or his pockets or his computer, were because I would intuitively suspect when the Grey One had escaped the control of the Reverend.

I would long to not find any evidence to confirm my suspicion. But I always did. Suspicion did not disappoint.

> *Nothing shocked me anymore; but little did I know that the Grey One had not reached his limits. Far more harrowing episodes were to come.*

I can recognise him in an instant, when things appear grey that is where he pervades, where things are not clear or not quite making sense. The non-committal middle ground between reasonable and irrational is where the Grey One's influence is at its most persuasive.

There were two specific dreams I remember and one interesting occurrence, all around the same time.

I dreamt we were at a wedding, a significant family wedding. When the photographs were developed, the Reverend and I were completely naked... You may laugh...we did!

It wasn't wasted on me. I knew exactly what the dream interpretation was. I didn't need to mention it to anyone else.

Nakedness equals nothing hidden, no secrets, nothing covered up and all the flaws are revealed. The photograph of someone or something in print is called an exposure. In the process of development, a film is exposed to light. An exposure is the disclosure of something that cannot be seen prior to exposure. Or the intensity of light on a film. Also being abandoned without clothes leaves us exposed and vulnerable.

The Reverend dreamt that he was in our bathroom attempting to clean up the filthy dirty mess that was overflowing from the toilet. The more he tried to clean it away the worse the mess overflowed. I am sure I don't need to share the interpretation here. It was obvious.

Oh, how we were warned!

Then in real life, not a dream, I kept finding a frog on my front doorstep. Three times I was leaving the house to go out and there it would be, on my doorstep. I mentioned it to a friend, as it was very unusual for this to happen three times in the same place, within a few days.

Instantaneously, my friend responded.

"Maybe it's a sign your Prince will come."

Earlier I wrote that I felt like the Princess who got her Prince. Who will kiss the frog so that I can have my Prince back...?

Time to reflect ...

Don't lose hope, my friend, keep looking and hoping for change. I am still looking and hoping with you. So are many others, stuck on a similar wheel of misfortune, wondering if it will ever stop?

Hope is the optimistic expectation of good.

Would you want the alternative? I wouldn't, hopelessness is agony, and it abandons all belief in success. I am sticking with hope every day.

I put messages of hope all around me, so my mind would be drip-fed with the belief in and expectation for good days ahead. These messages changed over the years, but I never lost hope, even when the signs grew worse.

Be inspired, there are more stories like ours out there.

You and me, we need to talk about them, to create a circle of hope all around the world.

Begin now. Put recipes of hope on your menu every day.

Pray...

Father, I ask you to awaken or reinvent hope where it is lost, or good has been given up on. Turn despair and desperation around now and sow seeds of hope into this life.

Amen

Recipes of Hope

Romans 15:13

May the God of hope fill you up with joy, fill you up with peace, so that your believing lives, filled with the life-giving energy of the Holy Spirit, will brim over with hope!

(The Message)

Lamentations 3:21

Oh, how well I remember – the feeling of hitting the bottom. But there's one other thing I remember, I keep a grip on hope.

(The Message)

Reverend Grey

Scene 6

The Elephant – Which Elephant?

Let us not be guilty of turning a blind eye,
In denial of how deadly the plague really was.
When it has completely destroyed us!

I would encourage everyone to look out for one another's Internet health care. Also, mental health is often a key factor in a dependency that leads to addiction.

As I am not a health care professional I can only relate my experience. It is because of my long-term personal experience that it has become instinctive in me to spot certain patterns of behaviour.

I have very strong reference points that may indicate a problem of sorts exists.

This won't signal what area the problem is in, how serious it is or how deeply it has affected an individual. Sensitivity is vital, not jumping to conclusions is essential, but it is equally important to raise the issue and not ignore it. And definitely do not conceal evidence that is uncovered.

Generally there would be many clues flagged up in an individual's character, along with distinct outward signs, that a marriage is in difficulty, to alert concerns.

Not so with the Reverend or with our marriage, however. There were no obvious grounds to justify direct or specific questioning around the Reverend's private life.

Whenever the subject of pornography came up with his colleagues, he would often be the first in with a joke to make sure the subject didn't get personal.

The Reverend's performance, socially and professionally within his function, was never in question.

There are many subtle clues, if aware of where and what to look for, that over time may be recognised to flag up a possible problem with Internet pornography obsessions.

No one should want to keep this information quiet. Everyone should want his or her radar tuned to indicate the pollution of a secret pornography and / or sex addition, hidden behind passwords on obscure computer screens.

Significant personality traits will be similar in anyone who struggles with a secret addiction, obsession or compulsion. Beware though – the traits need to be recognised as long-term habits alongside others and appear to operate in corresponding situations rather than occasional or one off circumstances.

There may be a completely legitimate issue temporarily causing this behaviour, and allowances need to be made for such. More than two or three of the characteristics need to be regular practice, before any concern should be raised, as singularly they will be familiar to many of us.

In a relationship such as marriage or parent to child or even child to parent, no one should mind when sensitive questions are asked, when a problem is suspected.

Their initial response may be enlightening, though nothing is conclusive without actual evidence. If questions ruffle, or provoke uncharacteristic anger, or avoidance, uncomfortable and defensive mannerisms, there may be a cause for concern.

Note, that if there has been a long-term problem with pornography, positive response can be practiced in an effort to appear innocent.

The Elephant – Which Elephant?

Secret addictions are easy to conceal, especially around Internet pornography, sadly by the time the signs begin to show, the problem is far from the early stages.

You won't be popular for exposing a fascination to or with someone or something when it is first discovered. But keeping it in the dark feeds it, feeding it makes it stronger. The more it is exposed to the light through conversation and careful interest, the weaker it will become.

My experience is only in the area of Internet pornography and sex addictions through what I have experienced and observed through the Reverend.

There are the obvious signs that most of us are aware of, these have all been my observations for many years. Smart phones raised the bar to crazy levels of obsessive behaviours in my experience.

Mobile phones being constantly on silent and always in the pocket. Even taking it to the bathroom at times, which is normal for young people, but not for a married family man in his middle age. Personal grooming goes up a level in consistency and takes on a cleaner shaven aspect in every way and everywhere on the body.

Computer or device screens are positioned so that they cannot be viewed easily, allowing time to change their activity to emails or a work document when someone passes by.

Internet history is always deleted. Passwords and pass codes are withheld and access to all messaging apps are password protected. There would be a long list of the same mobile number bunched together to signal a messaging conversation on paper phone bills.

Most phone bills are paper free now so not so easy to detect unless it's possible to check the call history and messages on a phone.

I began to notice the Reverend was using free messaging apps that didn't show up on his bill. When I did get access to his phone and I discovered photos or messages, emails etc from the woman, I would send them to my own phone so that I had a copy in my own possession.

This was just something I did, then I transferred them all to a password protected app. Evidence is essential to confronting an addiction. I would never get a confession, however obvious the lie, if I didn't have the evidence to prove it.

Compartmentalising is very common in men, not so much in women. The Reverend was a serious case of compartmentalism. The difference in him was that the compartment where his secrets existed was totally detached from all other compartments. They should overlap and all relate in some way to each other.

This off the radar part that kept all his secret affairs and pornographic addictions didn't exist in his real lifestyle, it wasn't reality to him. This, we realised through counselling, was a symptom of the *dissociative disorder*.

Specific to the Reverend were some big giveaway clues that he was hiding his addictions.

He would be at work on his laptop at the dining table. I wouldn't be able to see the screen from where I would normally sit. I would hear him typing profusely, loudly and hurried. I would get up from my chair as quickly as possible to see he had stopped typing and was just looking at an email as if reading it.

The problem was, that same scenario would happen three or four times within half an hour, and he would still be viewing the same email when I looked at the screen.

I would ask who he was writing to or what he was typing, he would always answer that he had just sent an email.

The Elephant – Which Elephant?

Eye contact was difficult for the Reverend to maintain. Eyes reveal the soul of a person. Eyes are a window that reflect the heart, affections and motives of a person.

Then there were specific facial expressions, turns of his head and how he would stroke his face and head when he was uncomfortable. I admit there are times he would be uncomfortable for acceptable reasons and all of the above mannerisms would be seen, so the context of the discomfort is important to recognise.

More poignantly – their whole demeanour affects the atmosphere around them. This is the part that messes with your head and causes you to doubt your own mind and senses. All the physical signs that are so easily explained away do not explain what you feel in an atmosphere that you cannot touch but is just as real and as tactile as anything that is felt or smelt.

Some would call this our sixth sense; a deeply spiritual dimension that we are all created with, some of us are more aware of it than others. This is the facet of our humanity where God lives if we invite Him into it. If God isn't dwelling in that spiritual shape, other influences will rest there that create a dark aura around us. Enter my main character – Reverend Grey.

This is also where the 'Elephant in the Room' exists. A huge presence that no one wants to talk about, but cannot see past, but is totally non-existent to those who don't want to see or cannot see it.

On this matter, there needs to be caution.

This place, where all our non-physical senses come from, is also the seat of our emotions.

Our emotions are shaped by experiences and how they have impacted us for good or bad. Anything that triggers these senses will filter through our good, bad and / or damaged and unhealed emotions. Hearing the absolute truth out of this place takes a sifting process of many other factors. This is when we need others we trust to listen to what they hear, what they think, feel and understand.

For those who are in committed intimate relationships; if you have noticed that sexual arousal isn't happening the way it should, purely through intimate touch and nakedness. Are you finding that more of a porn star style approach is needed for arousal? If this is so, there may be an underlying pornographic issue creating this. Continued stimulation from pornography will eventually neutralise the ability for arousal any other way.

(Please be aware, arousal can naturally become more of a challenge with age!)

We were at a friend's house, with a small group of people. We were meeting for spiritual encouragement, transparency and accountability regarding our day-to-day lives as Christian people.

The question was asked to the group. "Which principles of biblical practice do we find difficult to obey?" I knew my response immediately,

> *Love is patient, love is kind...It does not dishonour others...It is not easily angered, and it keeps no record of wrongs. Love does not delight in evil but rejoices with the truth. It always protects, always trusts, always hopes, and always perseveres.*
>
> *1 Corinthians 13:4-7*

I didn't answer right away. I waited while others spoke to work out how I could choose words that didn't dishonour my husband.

How can any of us put all of that, all of the time, into practice? I was and still am tested in every part of it.

It's true we all will struggle to maintain those demands on love, but I was habitually being wronged on so many levels.

Scene 7

The Poison Chalice

Are you tired? Worn out? Burned out…?
Come to me. Get away with me and you'll recover your life.
I'll show you how to take a real rest.
Walk with me and work with me – watch how I do it.
Learn the unforced rhythms of grace.
I won't lay anything heavy or ill fitting on you.
Keep company with me and you'll learn to
live freely and lightly.

Matthew 11:28-30 (The Message)

The poison chalice weighed equally with the sweetness of my unconditional love for the Reverend. His two identities were becoming equal to each other. They had never been as proportionate as they were now.

The evidence that began to unfold more secrets over the next few years were far more serious.

Once they were in the past there was nothing I could do, but if they were in the future I would do my utmost to make sure they didn't happen.

The Grey One despised the light, he detested meeting the lovely other one of himself. If their worlds collided, it made him very uncomfortable, because they exist in conflict with each other. They are incompatible; it would be impossible to co-exist in agreement.

115

I was the only one who could force them to face each other, it wasn't pretty. No one else knew there was two of him, two completely opposing identities in one person.

I challenged the Reverend on every opportunity. I never let anything go without confrontation, and it made us both weary.

They battle, and the Reverend is weak against the deceptive Grey One.

We had moved again, to our seventh location since we married and were living in our fifteenth home. We relocated alone for the first time in twenty-seven years; this was a fresh start as a couple, not a family.

This position proved to be a great blessing to us both. Many loyal friendships and an opportunity for a career I loved that complimented the Reverend's role without difficulty.

Though sadly, it proved to be the area where my husband would make that one fatal attachment that he would not be capable of detaching from!

He risked everything for her, always believing he would get away with having his cake and eating it. Continuing to believe I would never expose him, but how much more did he consider I could take?

It was during this period he met 'her' — the person he is involved with.

The Reverend participated in street mission, which involved being on the streets until very late at night, which gave the Grey One the opportunity for promiscuity.

On more than one occasion he arrived home after 3am. I was at a loss of the energy to keep on surviving.

I knew he had been with her, without even knowing she existed at the time, because his reason for being so late didn't make any sense.

It was a Saturday evening that I saw an email on his computer. I find it unfathomable that he could reconcile engaging with extra marital sexual relationships on his phone or laptop at the same time as preparing to preach the gospel to a congregation the next morning!

This is the nature of addiction and dissociative disorder that became central to his character after many years of practice. He was by then numb to the impact on his conscience.

This discovery started a highly charged and volatile row between us, the anger in me raged. I threw whatever I could grab to throw at him. It was a very dark and sinister war between us.

Without warning I watched him go and pack his car to leave. This provoked the expected response, he knew I would not want him to leave. I begged, yes, can you believe it? I begged him not to leave, as this was still my greater fear.

If there had been a gun in the house one of us may have been shot that night!

He really could not manage his two identities when they clashed with each other. When I exposed the Grey One to the light of day the Reverend was weak and could not master him.

I couldn't master him either, but I could manage him. I had learned through past experiences that my anger and emotional stress made it impossible for the Reverend to manage his duel personalities when I had proved the Grey One's plot.

I knew what to do. I was able to steer the atmosphere, to enable the Grey One to escape back into the shade – as well as the

Reverend, I needed him to also retreat to the basement in this moment.

The car was loaded on the drive. The Reverend was about to leave, and he had no alternative as long as I continued in a confrontational and aggressive mood.

I needed to bring calm. I quieted my voice and asked him to sit down. We sat at the dining table facing each other. I spoke of my love for him, of the Reverend.

The prescribed pattern of learned behaviour to move the focus off the Grey One then switch focus to the Reverend, allowed the Dark One to retreat into obscurity. Once again the padlock of silence sealed the trap door, covered by the rug of secrets.

The Reverend unpacked the car. He didn't leave. I was relieved.

We had a very quiet night. I had reigned in my emotions and maintained calm.

The next day, on went our 'perfect life' and no one would have suspected what had occurred between us over the previous twelve hours. It was tough.

Since our move it had taken Reverend Grey no time at all to acquaint himself with more on line encounters, and with her he was to form a strong adulterous attachment too.

I continued to find on line messages of contact with both men and women. There were emails between him and many others, offering their desires and preferences of sexual activity with each other. I saw arrangements of meet ups, and all kinds of alternative and, in my opinion, perverted pornographic behaviours that I cannot describe. None of this was shocking anymore.

Eventually I discovered he had met up with others. Evidence of hotels and addresses where illicit sex was supposed to have taken place came to light.

The Poison Chalice

Registrations cards for sex clubs and condoms appeared in the car. Not for the first time.

I confiscated them. He could easily reregister and buy more condoms but I couldn't ignore them, even if I wasn't going to expose him.

The Reverend was planning to be at an outreach event. We shared a car at the time. At the last minute I arranged to meet a friend for coffee at the same time. I suggested I dropped him off at his event.

My suggestion was met with unexpected hostility and frustration. No explanation was given as a reason for his reaction. Testosterone multiplied as the Grey One drove us to his destination at ninety miles per hour on duel carriageways, screeching to a halt at roundabouts.

His anger was quite alarming. It was only in hindsight that I suspected the Grey One had sabotaged his time. The Reverend had no intention of attending the outreach event.

There would have been no time to cancel whatever arrangements had been made without my knowledge, meaning he was letting someone down. This is probably what made him so angry.

I suspect it was her he was planning to meet, the one who now pulls his strings.

On another occasion the Reverend left the house for a meeting. After saying his goodbye I passed by the laptop he had been using that morning to find a questionable website open. A message had been sent to an open forum on the site asking if anyone was free to meet that very morning.

I phoned him immediately, he answered his phone and I begged him in tears to come home and not to do anything stupid. He was very angry that I had found this out.

I was out of control with feelings I really cannot begin to explain. I would become much more familiar with those dark incomprehensible perceptions of intense emotional pain over the next few years. He arrived home shortly afterwards.

Anger was a very useful distraction to keep me at a distance that would quieten the scorn of my fury when he was caught in a lie or act of betrayal.

> *If all I had was evidence but no proof, that would provide the loophole to be used against me. I would have no option but to back off.*

One evening I had gone to bed early. I left the Reverend watching *Match of the Day*. I woke up in the very early hours of the morning to find he wasn't in bed. I came downstairs, as he would often fall asleep, only this time I discovered he was out.

There was no doubt in my mind where he was so late at night, but of course he had a feeble excuse for being out. I couldn't disprove his story so he stuck to his foolish lies.

The unpleasant cycle of discovery, confrontation, arguing, forgiving, apologies, and moving on wore me down.

I didn't realise at the time that there was no escape available to defeat this heavyweight in private.

We were in mortal combat with a militant hustler. I gave up the fight, I opted out of the contest, I gave up my husband to his immoral choices. I could not continue in conflict.

There is a huge difference between mistakes and wrong choices. It frustrates me when infidelity is called a mistake.

Mistakes are when there are no harmful intentions, but the result causes harm. Choices that are just plain wilful and wrong and

> *The Reverend was hooked on corruptions that were repellent; a wicked and repugnant stench contaminated our marriage.*

undoubtedly trouble or pain will be the outcome! These can never be called mistakes!

A year forward, I was still leaving him alone, not reacting to suspicions that were continually evident. I was getting on with life and turning a blind eye to all my imaginations. What was the point of doing or saying anything if I was never going to expose him?

I chose peace and quiet in the home over dispute and confrontations. Until about five years ago!

As a family we were organising a surprise party for the Reverend. Great lengths had been gone to, to make this a party of a lifetime, we had been organising it for six months.

We arrived, I was excited and nervous.

As he got to the venue, he recognised a few faces, then the double doors opened for him as our daughter sang out Tina Turner's *Simply The Best – Better Than All The Rest!*

She meant it as she sang it, he was one of the best.

He was totally overwhelmed, and emotional as he looked around to see so many familiar faces from the past as well as the present.

Our children did a wonderful job, the evening was an incredible success.

I made a closing speech honouring my husband the 'Reverend' for his excellent service to people, finishing with reciting a hymn of my husband's choice we sang at our wedding ceremony.

> *My goal is God himself not joy nor peace, not even blessing, but Himself my God.*

'Tis His to lead me there —not mine, but His – At any cost, dear Lord, by any road.

So faith bounds forward to its goal in God, and love can trust her Lord to lead her there.

Upheld by Him, my soul is following hard

Till God has full fulfilled my deepest prayer,

No matter if the way be sometimes dark,

No matter though the cost be oft times great,

He knows how I best shall reach the mark,

The way that leads to Him must needs be straight.

One thing I know I cannot say Him nay, One thing I do I press toward my Lord;

My God my glory here from day to day, And in the glory there my great reward.

Those words give me strength as I think of them now, as it was only weeks before the party that I discovered her – for the first time. The main cause of all my most recent suspicions and painful anguish!

Finding out my husband had not only been sexually unfaithful, but to conceive in my soul that he had allowed an emotional unholy soul tie to fester with her was harrowing.

> *He sacrificed our love on the altar of treason because his quest was for another.*

Adultery wilfully and maliciously burgles with intent leaving a family bankrupt and impoverished of stability and security.

It brought conflict to my own self-awareness and significance in our marriage. With choosing her he forced me into a battle. To win the awful war in my head I needed to arm myself with strength to consciously and intentionally crush the fear, inferiority and low self-esteem.

It was easy to say I was ready for waging war, but it was tough to believe I could win when it was far easier to surrender to the belligerent and aggressive enemy's worthlessness and uselessness.

Betrayal of this nature adjusts the settings in the mind.

This is when I unveiled the invisible Mr and Mrs Spencer! This was who they were online. I also discovered that they had been seeing each other quite regularly and had developed some kind of online partnership, soliciting themselves for group practices for more than a year.

They both assured me the relationship was over. It would obviously take time for me to believe that was true given the Reverend's history with the invisible Grey One.

Only a few weeks later I had a quick check of the Reverend's emails. He really wasn't very good at covering his tracks as I found out they had been together the day I was out with a friend and another day that I was in training all day.

I read an email from her recalling the time they spent together. I discovered which hotel they had met at, and how lonely she was when he left her. Her closing comment was recounting the details of their time together. Telling him how she wanted him to do the same 'hard core porn' with her next time they met. I was repulsed!

This was not an act that is consistent with loving intimacy. It was degrading and disrespectful and never would I have believed that my husband would give in to the Grey One to do this, had I not read it in black and white.

I am no prude. The Reverend and I enjoyed intimacy and the foreplay and climax of our lovemaking. If I had suggested anything involving the details I cannot divulge, he would never have complied! He was nothing but loving, gentle and tender towards me. Only the Grey One would do such a thing, I was never intimate with the Grey One.

I was somewhat relieved it was her suggesting he fulfilled degrading actions to her body. I have never evidenced anything that would accuse him of initiating anything similar.

I was so ashamed of him when I read the email describing what he had done to her, how can she have any self-respect, and how can the Grey One have any respect for her to degrade her that way? This is what I said at the beginning, much lust always wants more lust. What you had yesterday isn't enough for today, so the addiction demands more thrills, more ecstasy, more fantasy, more degradation and yes, more perversion.

He had gone to bed already. I ran upstairs feeling torn to shreds. He saw the look on my face, he knew instantly he had been found out. I was still heart sore from discovering their involvement with each other. I was anxious about going out of town for the day with a friend. The plans came into play as soon as my back was turned and the Reverend could not resist the opportunity of transition into the Grey One for a day.

He jumped out of bed full of apologies and remorse, we talked, he was sorry. Sadly, he was only sorry he had been found out and for the hassle it caused him.

Honestly, he selfishly and sinfully wanted it all. He wanted me and the family and all that comes with us, and her and the perversions that come along with her.

Time to reflect …

The events in this chapter span more than twelve months, during which I made a decision to ignore the Grey One for one year. I turned a blind eye. I forgave in advance and handed him over to his immoral choices. I was fed up of the contention. There was nothing more I could do. I was desperately sorry we had come to this point. Maybe if I stopped warring, he would run out of the energy a double life demands. It was my only option, as I knew we would be in continual conflict.

I had to find a way to survive the torment without losing a grip on my mind. I learned to focus on what was positive and good; I was determined to not lose myself in the pain. I refused to allow the Grey One to steal my smile, or trade my thankfulness for bitterness.

We can be in control of our own choices, but we cannot control the circumstances that are consequential to the decisions we make. One day something will happen that we hadn't planned for, and takes the control out of our hands and we become victims of our own devising.

Pray…

Father God, I pray now for anyone reeling from the agony of adultery and the awful consequences it brings. I pray now for healing and comfort to mind and emotions that are in turmoil. For the one who has nowhere to go and no one to talk to, draw yourself in to them, that they may feel your presence rushing over them like a blanket of love that distinguishes fear.

Psalm 34:4

God met me more than halfway;
he freed me from my anxious fears. (The Message)

Scene 8

Humpty Dumpty Fell Off The Wall

A dangerous character is as frail as Humpty Dumpty – when the Reverend falls over the edge it will take more than horses and men to put him back together again.

I adapted to the Reverend's duplicity in the same way our eyes adjust to darkness from light.

In my subconscious mind I provided the Grey One with an ally. He needed a wife with a framework that would defend him and manage his addictions.

Now I am all too mindful that I became regulated by faulty precepts in my head, because of the damage to my emotional and mental well-being by Reverend Grey. I have only had one marriage, which was extraordinarily exposed to the pollution of porn. I have no idea what a marriage with one hundred per cent trust, without betrayal and secrets feels like.

> *He was unable to watch as I agonised, I was alone in my sorrow.*

I was still his secret keeper. I had no one to talk to except the Reverend who was still under the control of the Grey One and so was I.

We are still four years from national exposure! Life was busy.

Reverend Grey

I was enjoying my career, learning well, equipping myself with a Diploma in the area of Youth and Children's development.

The highs and dreaded lows around Reverend Grey continued however.

Suspicions stacked up as they grew more discernible, but without evidence or proof to confront him. I knew the truth would never come out of the mouth of the Reverend. I signed up to one of the websites, not

> *What will he have left when he runs out of health, money and time I often wondered?*

with the same intentions as the Grey One, I wanted to see if I could find him.

It didn't take long to come across his profile. He worked more than one site with varying names. He had posted photographs, not of his face, but I recognised him, as his wife should. I made contact with him without him knowing it was me – he responded very quickly.

He was utterly charming and sympathetic to the reasons I fabricated for being on the site, I can see why he gets the interests of other users. Many who use these sites are troubled people with underlying emotional damage such as Reverend Grey suffered. He would appeal as one to make an attachment with because he was very keen to please. He offered his learned value of empathy as well as sexual favours of many descriptions, which he described with intimate detail. His strongest need and what gives him most pleasure was to please others, rather than be given pleasure.

I eventually sent him a photograph, not of myself.

As ridiculous as it was messaging my husband on an Internet dating site, I got so obsessed with watching how far he would go that I kept it going for months. I had nothing to gain from this bizarre exercise but more distress as I was witnessing first hand that my husband was having an on line affair with me without knowing it was me! He said I sounded really lovely and he liked me a lot! He pursued me for weeks to meet him, but I couldn't go that far.

He talked me into meeting up. It was planned that we would cheat on each other, with each other! It was so sickening to be part of the Grey One's secret life. It gave me no pleasure at all so I chickened out. I didn't want to know that he had actually turned up. I preferred to hope that he hadn't. That was the end of the exercise; it was never going to solve our problems only feed them.

The common thread that ran through all the messages, profiles and status updates of Reverend Grey, was that they were all about him pleasing others, what he could do for them. They were never about what he wanted them to do for him, or to him or what he needed from them. The emphasis and priority was always that he desired to give pleasure not demand it.

There were occasions in the Reverend's role when he had the privilege of spending time with high-ranking police officers in the county we lived in. The date was in my diary for an upcoming meeting with them and as I was free the day of this meeting the date was in both our diaries. The meeting venue was set in lovely picturesque surroundings near where we lived, and yet those well-known alarm bells were ringing loudly in my ears.

I had some work to do on an assignment so I suggested going with him to work in the car while he was in the meeting then we could go and have lunch together.

Suddenly, the Reverend became very aggravated and angry as the Grey One, who resented me spying on him and not believing him, emerged! Well there was no holding me back. I was going and unless he had good reason he was not going to stop me, hostile or not! I ignored his malice and kept my cool.

Reverend Grey

Had the Reverend been telling the truth, he wouldn't have got so angry. He never minded that I would travel with him when everything was truthful and genuine, he enjoyed my company.

I knew my intuition was telling me to go with him and was quite amused by the whole event. Surprisingly, I was able to smile at times when I witnessed the stupidity and foolishness of the Grey One's plans, I could see straight through him.

He has no idea how I can read him. He completely disregards female intuition when it's his own behaviour setting off the signals that something isn't right. Female intuition is a strong and mysterious quality, not to be relied upon without actual evidence, but will serve as a prompt that there is something that exists undercover needing to be uncovered.

We drove off to the meeting. He went inside. I got my laptop out and began working on the assignment. Within minutes, he was back in the car!! The meeting was rearranged! Surprise! Not to me.

Apparently he had been sent an email a few days before the meeting which he didn't receive. Naturally I didn't believe him. This was his style, to cause me to trust he is still going to a planned meeting when he knows rearrangements have been made which provided him with the opportunity to meet her.

Well, the lengths he went to in order to prove he was *genuinely* going to a *bogus* meeting – but he proved nothing except how stupid he was.

He actually commented that he had enjoyed our day together and the rest of the afternoon. My fuming days were mostly over; I knew this was my lot. I took small pleasure in ruining some of his plans in the years to come.

Too many people would be thrown into chaos by exposure. Many lives would be disrupted. I wanted to grow old with him, I could forgive him.

It was spring 2014; we were on our way home from a five day retreat. I downloaded emails.

I saw an email that made my heart miss a beat. From a 'Colin Churchgoer'. I can use that name as no such person exists. His name is not my fabrication to protect an identity, but their own fabricated name to protect them self.

The email subject read: You are a lovely lady, you deserve better.

The short message stated words to the effect; if the Reverend didn't resign from his position he would send pictures and profiles that he had taken from one of the websites the Grey One used and send them to the papers. Also attached were actual photos of him and the profile status the messenger threatened to disclose.

I replied the following day, telling him how I felt when I received his email. That it carried the impact he probably intended. As he was not divulging his true identity, I preferred not to enter into any more dialogue other than this reply.

I continued to say that if he was certain he was correct in his findings, to please, follow the biblical pattern to deal with it, as directed in Matthew 18:15-17. This way would protect our children from unnecessary humiliation. My children and I would appreciate this.

I heard from him once more. When I replied the second time the email bounced back undeliverable. The email account had been closed.

I would spend hours mulling things over and over in my head, what to say to the Reverend, following an exposure of adultery.

Sometimes I even believed I made things worse and would find myself apologising for doing so. How misguided and twisted had my mind become?

I began to use alcohol to take the edge off reality for the night, evenings were the most difficult. Daytime was fine as I had plenty of opportunities to distract my focus.

There were good days as well. I would feel some hope when he said we would survive this. I

> *The cast iron ball of sorrow that weighed heavily in my stomach and longed to be satisfied with love and comfort from the Reverend grew heavier.*

needed to hear him say it because alone I always felt there was little hope, so any hope he gave me I would hang on to.

Underlying anxiety increased during those years. Only the Reverend could change that.

I appreciate and am very thankful for the wonderful times we had. I always hoped they would come back as they should, not spoilt by violations.

Life ticked by happily for the most part, interrupted with some fractious times, but happy was my general disposition with many good distractions.

Then in May 2015 I found texting conversations that I watched for a week as they exchanged photos and terms of endearment and affection for each other and the use of strong sexual language that described what she wanted him to do to her and of course he couldn't wait. I was distraught, but I still remained silent, except I prayed, because I couldn't take anymore!

I wasn't giving up the fight.

The weekend that followed the Reverend was meeting a friend, who I knew, for a drink on a Sunday evening. I had seen all the messages between them that confirmed all the arrangements. Unknown to me however, the friend had cancelled during the afternoon. The opportunity was used to arrange to meet someone else, other than her, from another Internet site. I honestly don't know what happened on that occasion. He wasn't out of the house very long, so it was hopeful that nothing physical happened.

I found out the next day about the cancelled arrangement. Then I saw an unfamiliar text conversation of an arrangement to meet the person just mentioned! He had left our house full of children and grandchildren for his burning crime of lust. We had enjoyed a good weekend and Bank Holiday Monday that had been his birthday.

> *How could I possibly believe anything he said? Suspicion did its worst and yet more corrosion ate its way through our relationship!*

I had also discovered the messages during the previous week. I had kept the discovered texts to myself to get past the weekend and his birthday, because we had family staying with us to celebrate with their father. The trap door to the cellar was still securely locked by my silence, and my feet were firmly unmoved from the rug of secrets.

Then, with all the accumulation of pent up anger of the past week, adding to that the arrival on the scene of another suspicious character, I could not contain myself. I let him have it!

All the venom from the pain in the pit of my stomach of how I felt with his adulterous lies, just poured out of my mouth. I drank too much wine to dull the reeling pain, and I vomited!

I had at this point thought I would simply give up the fight to stay strong. The benefit of the doubt was not an option for my tormented mind, I instantly believed the worst!

Reverend Grey

It was the worst. I was reduced to torturing despair when it became a certainty that in his unseen private life, when no one was aware of our difficulties, Reverend Grey was involved in a full on affair with her, the woman he is now involved with. Their liaison had lasted for over three years at that time. I found out who she was, her name, where she lived, and her husband and children's names. I acquired her contact details from a Google search. She was aware I found all this out about her as we shared several messaging and email conversations.

I have many emails, messages and photographs she has sent to the Grey One over the years, she had used different names and email addresses. Now I know they were all one person, her.

On several occasions the Reverend would promise me it's over, but then after a few weeks I would find out that he hadn't been honest.

It was all becoming more unmanageable as I could feel the pain hitting the wall of near breakdown at my core.

My silence held me captive in a cell of cruel lies and deceit, which were now capable of gross ruin and destruction.

I was right on the edge of the most debilitating pain possible. I had done all I could do to stop this liaison, the most time they shared phone calls, texts and emails, but they, together have violated every moral boundary that exists to protect a marriage and a family.

The guns were ready to open fire. Who would pull the trigger to mark the day I feared? The day when the pain would pierce the wall and my marriage would be tested beyond its durability, to then unravel, though always believing we would piece back together for the sake of our love, our history and our family.

I was living in a continual torment of lies and deceit, doubt and suspicion, while he just lived his life of greed, lust and selfish calculations.

I was the innocent one, but for me to be free would mean ultimate loss.

I wrote to her.

She wrote back telling me how much she loved the Reverend, actually it's the Grey one she thinks she loves! She said she provides a distraction from the demands and pressures of his responsibilities and enables him to be the wonderful man he is!

I mentioned that I had prayed. It was a short prayer of desperation that ruptured from my broken heart. I was standing in my bedroom, erratic with anxiety, I simply said out loud, "God, I cannot take anymore." It was one of the most sincere prayers I had ever prayed. Instantly

> *I wonder how she feels now that has she assisted his demise and the complete breakdown of relationship with his whole family!*

these words ran through my head, "Move out of the way then." I said out loud, "Okay, I am moving out of the way."

Again, as I had before but now with a stronger conviction, I handed our outcome into the will of my Heavenly Father.

Had I really been in the way all these years? Yes I had. I had done too good a job of protecting my husband!

Time to reflect …

Instead of protecting my husband from exposure for as long as
I had, I should have allowed him to fail years before he did. It
was my own self-promoted role to be his minder and
bodyguard. Had he failed years before, we would have
recovered much quicker and without the depth of pain and
ultimate demise that we suffered.

I would not recommend that anyone do what I did, I was naïve
and in denial of how bad things were for a very long time.

I fear there are too many secret keepers out there, like me,
afraid of the cost and impact on family. It is daunting to stand
by and do nothing while watching your nearest and dearest
self-destruct. When I moved out of the way, it was my last
resort.

Pray…

*Father God, I pray now for 'Secret Keepers'. I pray they will
be brave and have the strength to step aside from the role of
minder over the wrongs of their loved one. I pray they will trust
you who can make something wonderful out of their biggest
mess. I pray that from now on they will begin to lean on you,
knowing you are a perfect father who makes everything
beautiful in his time.*

You Make Me Brave

*I stand before You now
The greatness of your renown,
I have heard of the majesty and wonder of you.
King of Heaven, in humility, I bow.*

*You make me brave
You call me out beyond the shore into the waves.*

Humpty Dumpty Fell Off The Wall

You make me brave.
No fear can hinder now the love that made a way
As Your love, in wave after wave
Crashes over me.
For You are for us, You are not against us
Champion of Heaven
You made a way for all to enter in.

I have heard You calling my name
I have heard the song of love that You sing
So I will let You draw me out beyond the shore
Into Your grace, Your grace.

Bethel Music

Reverend Grey

Scene 9

Step Away From the *Trap* Door

I believed in you, I trusted you to be true,
I didn't know when I looked deeply into
your beautiful brown eyes,
They were telling me so many lies.

The Reverend promised that he had ended all contact – blocked her number from his phone, and eventually we moved on and had a great summer.

For almost three months there was no suspicious behaviour, no discoveries of betrayal. I felt strong, without anxiety or fear. Had my husband at last realised he was walking on very thin ice?

He may have, but the demon lust doesn't let anyone off the hook that easily!

Tuesday August 25, 2015, is a day my family will never forget!

We were at a Christian festival, arriving early as always with those involved in setting up and preparing for the event.

The Reverend was busy getting on with his responsibilities, the children and grandchildren along with some friends gathered together for lunch. The Reverend joined us but didn't eat. He was quiet; we hadn't noticed him leave to get back to task.

Later that afternoon the Reverend came to find me. I was alone. He sat down and said he had something to tell me, he looked 'grey'!

Reverend Grey

I knew something was seriously wrong!

I braced myself for impact as he gave me an email to read.

It took over three decades for the brakes to be applied. The duel-controlled life was stopped at last. Their paths had crashed head on.

> *I stepped aside as the Rug of Secrets was removed, the padlock unlocked and the basement door was flung open!*

The Reverend was exposed of his deceptions and the Grey One his deeds. There was no guarantee which one of them would relinquish command to the other.

After many years of anticipating the moment in the space of a few hours everything changed.

The Reverend was disqualified from his position. His credentials were under threat as his deep, dark, private behaviour was exposed in a most cruel and destructive way.

There was never a moment where I had to lie for my husband over the years. No one would ever have had a reason to question his morals.

To most, all they saw was a kind, generous, thoughtful and funny man, who loved his wife and family and cared for those fortunate as well as the less fortunate. That person still breathes, but he is in chains, and the Grey One still holds the key... for now.

I knew nothing about the circumstances of this exposure – a very similar context to what I received fifteen months prior to this one.

It was revealed by a different yet equally creative name which again had been chosen to conceal a true identity. I don't know for sure, but I suspect it was the same person as Colin Churchgoer.

Just as before, screen shots had been taken of explicit conversations the Grey One had been involved in over the summer of 2015, along with photos of himself, including his head and shoulders.

They were collectively emailed to newspapers and a number of organisations that the Reverend was well known to. So not only the newspapers as threatened before.

It appears to me someone who had been on the same sites recognised the Reverend and decided to cruelly expose him by distributing an email that explained who he was and saying that he shouldn't be allowed to continue in his positions, with such questionable morals.

A corrupt and unethical plot detonated the grenade that had lay on my doorstep for years and was not handled with care by the person who pulled the pin. The brutal force blasted through our lives to result in a big mess, as any explosion would, and left casualties in its wake.

This was the moment I knew we would face one day. But never in my wildest dreams did I think someone could be so vengeful, spiteful and merciless to my husband and especially his family.

A faceless accuser, guilty of the same transgressions, callously brought my home to ruins. In public display for all to see we were blown up, desolate and torn to pieces.

Again – this was another damning outcome of our own neglect to speak up. We don't know whose hands our shameful wrongs will fall into.

I hoped with all my heart the Reverend would at last master control, but sadly the Grey One disqualified him, defending his own mastery by using shame as a weapon to stab wounds of abjection and degradation into the already torn flesh of his opponent's emotions and mind.

In his bleeding and dying shame the Reverend surrendered to the Grey One, stuffing as much of him back into the basement as he could, locking him away out of view, hidden again from sight.

The Reverend was far too fragile for honesty and transparency at that time.

I never imagined it would happen this way. The fact that it was sent while we were at the festival was intended to cause maximum humiliation. I cannot begin to imagine what that violent and appalling exposure did to him. However terrible our sins, grace will craft humiliation into celebration and the Holy Spirit will design beautiful artistry with the ink stains of our shame when we come before Him.

Yes, this day needed to come, and yes, the person was correct that the Reverend should not be allowed to continue in his role, but he should have been exposed privately and in a biblical manner!

The greater the bomb, the more professional expertise is required from the bomb disposal squad.

The Reverend's grave misdeeds fell into the hands of an immature and unskilled buffoon who was blinkered towards disclosure, forsaking respect and courtesy for the family and community he devastated.

The Reverend spoke to his children first, and then procedures were implemented.

Unbeknown to the person whose intention it seemed was to gain maximum humiliation for the Reverend, we were surrounded by sixteen members of our family and many close friends who supported us unconditionally!

I felt that we couldn't have been in a more loving and caring environment. We were in a bubble of love and protection for a whole week.

It was a disgraceful way the individual chose to expose the Reverend. There was no other intention but to ruin him. He needed help, not humiliation. The intention of exposure should be to restore, not to ruin. The well-being of an individual and especially their family, should be of paramount importance.

Removing the Reverend from his pastoral position was only one part of the process. I wonder if the perpetrator who committed this awful act against him, is also living a double life resulting in another secret keeper protecting them.

> *It is never ok to destroy someone who struggles with pornography or any other addiction.*

I was about to find out who my true friends were, and I am humbled and blessed to find I have many wonderful friends who have loved me and my family and cared for us sacrificially and generously for the past year and more. Not one person I count as a friend has let me down.

I was shocked that while I had believed things were improving over the summer, the Grey One was still grooming on line with physical, sexual intentions.

I was truthfully able to say to my family and friends that I knew nothing about that specific site. Some asked if there was more, but I wasn't able to answer that question then. Of course there was more. I needed to give the Reverend the opportunity to bring the Grey One completely into the light himself!

There's advice in the bible that says, *"Confess your wrongs to each other and support each other, so that you can live together whole and healed,"* James 5:15 (my paraphrase).

Reverend Grey

I believed there is no healing in confessing other people's wrongs, unless they have broken the law! It will only cause more pain.

I needed to give the Reverend the opportunity to confess all of his other entanglements, to his family. I was aware of most of them, but his children had no idea of how immoral their father had lived.

The fact that someone else chose to confess the Reverend's improprieties in a publicly humiliating way has caused a lot of pain for his innocent family.

Needless to say, the sender of the email kept his or her identity a secret. I believe their identity will come to light someday. He or she cannot control the circumstances around the choices that they made. Circumstances do and will happen eventually.

Every day a life changing event that creates havoc may occur, that we haven't foreseen or been forewarned of. We survive, just as we did the last time and we will again. We become a different person each time harrowing information or violations take us out from our blind spot. It throws our world upside down, and when we finally come to ground, we are not the same as we were before.

Two things in life shape us; what gives us pleasure and what gives us pain are the experiences that can serve us with the opportunity to become bitter or better!

Lust, addiction, seducers, the Grey One, those ugly websites and her, enticed my husband from me. I tried everything to prevent us from losing him. It was a pointless battle, because he didn't want to be prevented. He went fishing in a muddy stagnant lake every day and finally he got pulled in and now he's struggling in the debris.

We can look at other people's lives and wish we were them, that we had their life, their marriage, their job, money, house and possessions.

I'm sure there were those who looked at the Reverend and me, believing we really had the 'perfect life'. It was obvious that we were in love, we were a good team, and we were successful and happy, which we were. We faced every hurdle, of which there were many, and jumped them, not realising, however, how fragile our marriage was.

Every person, every couple, every family have grim experiences and lifelong relentless circumstances and conditions that have to be managed.

We can all have those moments, when we look at other people wishing we had what they have. We have to realise there are realities about their lives that we know nothing of. We are better off settling for who we are rather than swapping our mess for someone else's.

We will not be equipped to cope with other people's chaos. All our challenges begin small as we grow. With every challenge we learn to slowly align. By the time the worst overtakes us, we will have strengthened our resilience to cope with it. As each trial comes and goes, it prepares us for the next one.

Our mess is our mess. It makes us who we are. We can be stronger for it. This is why it is so important to embrace the life we have. Be grateful for the wonderful. Change for the better where it's possible, and then bravely manage the mess that we can do nothing about.

The festival was over. It was time to go home. What had been our normal for over thirty-three years was over. We had a process to live through to find what was unknown to us.

Time to reflect ...

Our brand new normal!

In times like this when shocking things happen, stay safe, remain with people who will love you and protect you. To be alone is the worst thing. If a person is injured and bleeding everywhere and groaning loudly with pain, we tell them to sit or lie down, while medical professionals stem the blood flow and bandage them up. Physically they need time to let their system do its work as they respond to shock. Plus the blood makes a mess and the world doesn't need to know they're in pain.

Be careful who you confide in, choose your friends wisely, choose who hears your pain and sees your tears. For the rest of the time, dry your eyes and smile.

Pray...

Father God, for those who are facing their mess or troubles of which there are many, who are walking into unchartered territory, I pray they will not fear what may be ahead but they will go forward in confidence that you know the end of the story and you are in control.

Amen

Isaiah 41:10
Don't panic. I'm with you.
There's no need to fear for I'm your God.
I'll give you strength. I'll help you.
I'll hold you steady; keep a firm grip on you.

(The Message)

Scene 10

Ghost Train

All the skeletons are out of the darkness,
We made it to the end of the ride.
Then up from the floor lurks the biggest fright of all.

With one successful career ended, another successful career under scrutiny, the Reverend found work that would not be impacted in any way by the exposure.

This was both a good and bad thing; good because it kept us financially solvent, bad because the Grey One had opportunity to disassociate and meet her.

She was the one he chose to confide in while he was at work. When I learned that he was entrusting his grief and pain with her it was a bitter pill of rejection to swallow.

In the evenings alcohol was enough to dope me, thankfully it doesn't take much to induce a drowsy effect with me. Then to wipe me out completely I would take sleeping tablets that I bought on the Internet mixed with anything else in the house that would cause

I was weak in the struggle against my own demons. I wanted to sleep; I didn't want to wake up. Hear me! I wanted to sleep — I didn't want to die...

147

drowsiness. I always made sure they were available. This had been my increasing practice for five years.

After dropping my husband off at the train station as he went to his new job, along with my morning cuppa I would pop down more medication to induce sleep.

I would set my alarm to wake me up in time for any appointments I had that day. I would sleep till the alarm sounded, then I would get up, shower, tidy the house and go out, giving an appearance of health and happiness. If I had nothing planned I would sleep all day and get myself ready for when my husband came home.

Thoughts that had plagued my mind many years ago began to re-surface. I would be driving and it would cross my mind to drive head on into a brick wall.

That was the only thought of that nature I was troubled with. There was no way I wanted to injure or kill myself, I had too much and too many people to live for and I knew I would eventually have a brighter future ahead.

Our children continued to ask subtle questions about their father's morals, all I would say was that they needed to ask him those questions, not me. Of course this answer from me meant there were questions that needed answers.

> *The Reverend and I were readjusting to a colossal life change, but we were not leaning on each other.*

He was speaking to and seeing her, but he denied it. He also denied that he was on any pornographic or dating websites.

Then the expected decision was made. The Reverend's credentials would be removed with immediate effect. He was no longer a Reverend. He had been disqualified.

The Reverend and I had given over three decades to a calling and job that we both loved, and had now lost following the exposure of a lifestyle of the Grey One's sexual addictions.

He was still my husband, and father to our kids and papa to all the grandchildren, but he was still lying to us all. In doing so he was gradually disqualifying himself from our lives.

He was still the Grey One. His Grey grew even darker. It seemed he felt safer in the darkness with the Grey identity than he did with honesty, because truth made him vulnerable.

He would never defend a lifestyle with such double standards for anyone else. How could he be so blind to think the rules were different for him?

As a young Reverend in his twenties, he was shocked by the marriage of a woman in our congregation. He looked after her and cared for her while supporting her through a divorce. She was a woman in her sixties or seventies. Her husband had been involved in an affair with another woman for many years; she lived not far from where he had lived with his wife. He was sleeping with his mistress every night, but going home to his wife to get fed. This was his habit every day. The Reverend was outraged at his arrogance and the disrespect he showed his wife and daughter.

Now in 2016 as I am writing this down...

Though the circumstances are different, he has become that man.

He is today, and every day, causing intolerable suffering and distress by his dishonour and disloyalties as we are forced to bear the betrayals of his abandonment and rejection of his marriage and family.

I am so confused right now, as he is not an unkind or mean or rebellious person. I can only equate his behaviour with spiritual deception or blindness, or mental illness, such as depression.

Then I was asked the big question by one of my children. I was taken by surprise with the direct approach; there was no subtlety woven through their words.

"Has dad ever been with anyone for sex who he had met online?"

I could not lie; there was no skirting around the truth. No opportunity to blag my way out of this one. Even if I had not answered, apart from the fact my eyes welled up with tears, my face told the truth. Silence alone would have been an answer to such a direct question! Of course my honest answer required more questions.

> *Though I said I would never expose the Grey One, I could not lie for him. For the first time, I had done it. . . . I had opened up my mouth.*

I was unprepared for this impossible position. I could not lie to our children.

All the hidden mysteries behind the scenes of the Grey One's unseen story were now exposed to his much loved children.

I had arranged to see my daughter the next morning. She knew instantly something had changed and that it wasn't good news. What a week for my family. They were loved and supported by their spouses as their relationship with their father fell apart. Relationships were at an all-time low between them and their dad.

My parents had planned to visit for a few days the same week our children found out their father was living a double life on a far larger scale than they first knew. With him being involved in an affair with her for as long as he has.

> *Little did we know things would still get worse.*

This was a tricky week as it was... Then my parents arrived for a four day visit. I didn't want them to know anything unless they needed to. If my mum has a reason to worry to the point of robbing herself of sleep, she wouldn't refuse the opportunity. My puppy got lots of walks, so that I could talk to the family daily, they were devastated beyond words.

There were no words that would put together the foundations that had just disintegrated from beneath their feet.

I don't know if I fooled my parents, probably not! They were far too polite and appropriate not to meddle. I'm sure they sensed things weren't okay...especially when events such as this happened.

We all went for a day out together. My parents, my daughter, her two youngest children and me. We drove past the car-parking place where the Grey One parked his car each day near the train station. The grandchildren pointed out Papa's car with excitement. We continued to enjoy the day out. When driving home a few hours later we drove past the same car park and my father noticed the car wasn't there!

My heart plummeted, my tummy rolled with the threat of a tsunami, I was nauseous. His car should have been there for another two hours or more. It was only three in the afternoon; he wasn't due home until five thirty. Suspicion prompted me of the possible events. He jumped on the train at lunchtime, used his car to visit a hotel room or at least meet her, and then when he came back to the car park his space had been filled so he parked elsewhere. Then he hopped on the train back to work. A long lunch break yes, but he would have worked on the train journeys.

He may not have imagined us driving past the same place twice. It wouldn't have dawned on him to even consider we might drive past there once. Of all the weeks when the children discover their father's affair, it becomes a reality to our daughter as she saw his car, then she saw his car mysteriously gone! My parent's left. It was time to let the Grey One know that his children knew about his affair and all the other sexual behaviours he was caught up in.

He was very angry with me. He felt like he had been exposed all over again, sadly, he had. Surely, I asked myself, he didn't expect me to lie for him, when there had never been a reason to lie before? There had never been a situation that demanded I tell a direct lie to protect him. I could justify remaining silent, but I couldn't justify speaking lies.

The burden of enduring anxiety would rise and fall depending on how reliable his plans were in a day. If I was with him, they were my best days, because if I was with him, that was my favourite place, right by his side, the only place I could find calm in the centre of unrelenting and unbearable turmoil.

The exposure in August raised many questions. We were both so wrong to have kept these secrets, because I am not doing so any longer it's as though I am betraying him.

She would regularly interrupt our times together with messages and photographs. There was some comfort in between the moments of pain she caused in that he was with me.

It was me he saw last thing at night and first thing in the morning as we slept together.

For many years my faith in the Reverend's ability to defeat the Grey One and bring him to an end has been at rock bottom. He is still surrendering to the Grey One's whims and fantasies. I have felt the loss of hope and belief in him sifting his soul to sort out his morals for a very long time.

One day I sincerely hope he will see that he alone holds the key to the first steps into his freedom and find the strength to turn the lock and walk away from the person he has become. Only then can his family and his God intervene.

> *He is his own most powerful enemy against himself.*

There is nothing anyone can do until he makes a choice to get out of the place that he made a choice to get into.

There is no handle on the other side of the trap door, he must turn it, then cut the ties completely with everyone and everything that has kept him in the basement, in fantasyland. Only then will he be able to become the person he truly is: Handsome, Born of Fire and Gift of God, the one I deeply love and have lost...

At this moment, writing this chapter, it has gripped me unexpectedly, I am overwhelmed with grief and abandonment and extreme loss. I am so very cross with him for choosing adultery and lust over his children and me.

He boasts of our wonderful family and friends. They are wonderful and amazing. But his boast is that without him I can run into them and I have, they cannot replace him, however. They cannot be there in the middle of the night for a spontaneous hug and reassuring words of love and comfort. That's his place. He vowed to be that person for me. He has cheated me, sold me short of his promise.

How dare he conveniently deceive himself to believe it is the right choice to bail out of his responsibilities? That this is the best option for us? How did he come to the blind conclusion that we are better off without him?

We vowed to each other our loyalty and commitment. It is not okay that he deserts us for another. Who is she that she thinks it is acceptable to stealth a husband, father and grandfather who is the head of his family? Who is the man that allows this to happen? These feelings will pass, they do and will continue to come and go for the foreseeable future.

At this moment of writing I am angry and broken that my husband would do this to us. He is a Christian man and he knows he is morally and spiritually violating so many people and he is plain wrong.

I fully understand the humiliation he suffered and his need to hide for a while. He could have done that within the safety and love of his family. My husband is an intelligent man, as much as I concur with the effects of his early emotional traumas his behaviour is without excuse.

Now that rant is of my chest… I love him. I can't help it. I have given up trying to force myself to get over him.

We all stood by him and loved him beyond his demise. He was far more than the Reverend to us.

As a family our situation grew worse. Our children had only just found out about the affair. The situation was volatile and in an unresolved atmosphere of hostility between us our children arrived at our door.

In an instant, the Grey One vapoured and their father greeted our children with an effort of normality.

Their response was direct and confrontational as to how 'not normal' things were. The Grey One was backed up against the wall.

He didn't walk; he didn't talk either while our children begged him to choose his family. To fight for us.

I was horrified to hear one of my children say that we are dysfunctional as a couple and their father has been abusing me for years. That shocked me. I never saw it like that.

There were tears and disbelief in the person their father was. They had never seen this person before. They didn't know him or recognise him as dad. Yet another blindsided crash for our family.

They had never met the Grey One before. He was very familiar to me. But he was not ready to expose the full extent of the Grey One's violations.

> *The anger in my son was tangible; he shook his head saying, "I don't know this man."*

We expected him to run into us, so that we could all recover together. Counselling was offered and paid for by the organisation he worked for, which we both needed and was a big help over the next few months. But the Grey One became more dominating.

After our children left in anguish, their father said, "They're great kids." Why did he not say that when they were here?

Father and family would be estranged from one another for many weeks from that night! To say things were difficult was an understatement! The Grey One just got on with working.

He was attending counselling which was enlightening regarding the reasons, not excuses, for his behaviour. It must be said my husband never excused his moral flaws. He knew his behaviour was wrong and he knew he caused pain, but he was compelled to give in to his addiction to pornography, illicit sex and now her.

He continually took the chance that I wouldn't find out so in his mind, what I didn't know didn't affect me. Suspicion never left me, it was punishing me daily whether I knew any details or not.

The Grey One continued to find comfort outside of his marriage and family. We talked very little. He felt with family estranged that he might as well move out, that we would all be better off without him. He began to look for an alternative home. I was not ready for this. I was ok with it, then I wasn't, but really I wasn't!

I was putting up a united front believing we would survive. Never in a million years would I have believed it possible for my husband to leave us. With the rift between our children and their father growing further apart, the Grey One continued his plan to leave. What an awful, dreadful time that was. I was broken, very broken, that the Grey One had totally hijacked my husband.

> *I wanted our marriage to survive for a better than ever relationship.*

Not only had the Grey One obliterated the Reverend, he was intent on obliterating him as a husband, father and grandfather.

I would check almost every day that his car was where it was supposed to be parked, for my peace of mind. I was living on high alert always on vigil making sure he was where he was supposed to be. Family could not believe I still wanted him after all the harm he had caused. They wanted me to leave first, to take control, but I couldn't, it was not what I wanted to do. They were angry and that was to be expected.

There was nothing I could say in favour of their father that they were willing to accept or even listen to. Reverend Grey's recklessness stretched me to the point of fracture, crushing my fragile cerebral bones over and over again.

Every time I found that he had strayed into websites and / or adultery, I refused the option to get help, because I feared the outcome if I let as little as one other person know the secrets in our cellar.

The Grey One continued to look for a flat, while confiding in her. My children were telling me to leave their dad, but I wasn't ready. He was the man I want to be married to.

> *The next few weeks were the most unbearable of my entire life...*

Time to reflect ...

When those dark thoughts of driving into a brick wall at speed began to leap from nowhere into mind again, I did what I had done many years before. I quoted and applied God's word,

We demolish arguments and every pretention that sets itself up against the knowledge of God, and we take captive every thought and make it obedient to Christ.
2 Corinthians 10:5

That sorted them again. I took the thought and surrendered it to Christ. Gone!

I didn't have the energy to discipline myself through the misery of sleepless nights. Now in the present I don't need anything to help me sleep. It was a temporary dependency; the need for it no longer exists.

Pray...

Father, I pray for freedom from dark thoughts, where thoughts of self-harm invade the mind. I take authority over every thought that goes directly against your will and purpose. I make them obedient to your design.

In Jesus' name I demolish every evil hold or temptation that threatens harm.

Amen

2 Corinthians 10:4-6

The world is unprincipled. It's dog-eat-dog out there!

The world doesn't fight fair. But we don't live or fight our battles that way – never have and never will.

The tools of our trade aren't for marketing or manipulation, but they are for demolishing that entire massively corrupt culture.

Ghost Train

We use our powerful God-tools for smashing warped philosophies, tearing down barriers erected against the truth of God, fitting every loose thought and emotion and impulse into the structure of life shaped by Christ.

Our tools are ready at hand for clearing the ground of every obstruction and building lives of obedience into maturity.

(The Message)

Reverend Grey

Scene 11

Photo Shopped

The mask had slipped, but still it did not fall,
The cracks revealed the scars, but sadly not them all.

The separation continued to be planned for. My husband had found a flat, and it was a week until he moved out.

I was sick in my stomach at the thought of it. I could not accept that this would happen. I refused to believe it would. Surely at the last minute he would choose to fight for his family? I did not want him to leave me, this had to turn around.

It was a Tuesday evening, my husband was out with many of his friends from the local area. He had a good time and felt welcomed.

The next evening he met his counsellor, it was a turning point session. He welled up to cry as he was telling me his counsellor gave him hope. Hope was a quality he had lost.

The duplicity of his personality and lifestyle was tearing us apart and had been for years.

It was Friday, the last day before the weekend that was going to swallow me into abandoned despair and the unknown of separation. I was unprepared.

I had never lived alone; I grew up in a big noisy family, then grew a big noisy family of my own. This could be either a horrible, emotionally charged weekend or a hostile one. My emotions were on the edge of either and I was not in a place to anticipate either of the two parallels.

I knew my husband hadn't any plans of his own.

I booked two tickets to go and see the new James Bond movie. It was the right choice as we were able to spend the evening together without talking, except for my husband educating me about the model of the Bond car! Also, it was late when we arrived home so no time for a long drawn out conversation that may lead to an upset. We had a short warm chat and a drink then off to bed, we were surprisingly intimate. I felt cherished.

Saturday morning he suggested we went for a drive to a farm shop café for a coffee. We sat chatting superficially while waiting for our food to be served. Then between breaths the silence broke and he began to talk.

What he said took me completely by surprise! He reached for my hand and spoke words I had been longing to hear.

My husband had returned!

He explained that at some point through the previous week he had turned a corner. He wasn't sure when it was, the curry night with the guys, a successful counselling session, then seeing family for the first time in weeks, then our night out together – something fell into place. He continued saying he felt as though he has been lost at sea without an oar or a life jacket, and now he felt hopeful for the first time since the dreadful shaming email incident.

He thanked me for standing by him and asked me to forgive him, assuring me he loved the children and me and chose our future and us together.

I cried, he cried, the worst was over, I thought!

Sadly, the Grey One was not going to give up that easily. My husband continued counselling and changed his mobile number to stop unwanted contact.

He kept the same email address explaining it was the address that his work contacts used so would prevent him getting business. I had no choice but to accept that, but it did leave a vulnerable entry point to the Grey One.

The next day he emailed his children to let them know his decision.

He said he was sorry for putting them all through a terrible time the last few weeks and deeply regretted his actions that led to the unmasking of his other self, which gave ammunition for someone to expose him. Hopefully, he continued, we could all rebuild and continue to be the great family we are despite his deep flaws.

Over the following weeks we grew stronger and happier than, as you can imagine, we had been for a long time. I felt confident I was winning my husband's affections back.

I felt his desire for me return. I saw him looking at me with affection in his eyes; I hadn't seen that for a long time. I didn't see guilt.

There is something about the way a person looks at the one they love that is very unique. I would know when things were not going well for him when the affection had gone from his eyes. Affection was replaced by avoidance, shame and guilt, which couldn't be hidden.

Sadly, the Grey One still had the upper hand. He wasn't given the same message as us, therefore he stood his ground. The Grey voice silently mocked with the tone of foreboding evil: "We have been here before, I'm not going anywhere."

A year forward and I found he had begun grooming online again, to meet total strangers for behaviours I cannot describe.

For years for me to go out in the evening and feel assured my husband would be faithful, I had to know what he intended doing with his time. It was most reassuring for me if he arranged to be out with a friend who I knew and could confirm he was with him.

Now it should have been different, as he had very recently recommitted himself to fidelity. I was going out with a group of girl friends to the theatre. I was somewhat anxious about it because it was the first time trust was being put to the test since his change of heart and direction a few weeks before.

He had given me his word he was going to relax and watch some television. About ten minutes before I left, he went to the bathroom, with his phone. This was the worst thing he could have done, as he knows that triggers fear.

I asked for his phone.

I was apprehensive because I knew there would be Grey intent threatening to ruin my evening.

What a fool! He had texted someone very dubious, however it wasn't her. His face had the expression of a child caught in a lie as I looked at the message. The content of the message didn't imply a betrayal, but it was still alarming as it wasn't innocent in its subject.

I never want to see that look of shame again, or that naughty schoolboy face.

I went out anyway, but the evening was mixed with fear as well as smiles and laughter.

He would always deny there was anything he needed to admit to but I knew he was guilty because I saw it in his eyes. But for now, back in the make belief of a fresh start, I was hanging in there – but not naïve, we were still very close to ruin.

It was Christmas, he excelled himself with gifts. I know my children, family and friends who know his flaws were concerned for me. Worrying that I would overlook too many violations.

Photo Shopped

Looking back, I was as blind to the severity of his flaws as he was. Neither of us had really considered how messed up he really was. And in many ways I was messed up too.

This, I am convinced, was because my husband was wonderful in so many ways – it totally confused my thinking and sense of reality!

We had a fabulous Christmas Day with the family.

Next day, Boxing Day, we went to a party. I found a seat where I felt comfortable. My husband, of course, was more sociable and introduced himself to the people he didn't know, then pointed to me and remarked flippantly why I didn't get up from my seat!

My recent belief in him ebbed, I was losing him again. I didn't show it, or tell anyone. The secret keeper was still alive and well, too.

He was joking of course, but it was insensitive of him, as so many people there knew about his betrayals against me. He didn't let me down, he let himself down. I didn't say anything, but later that evening we talked about it and he said he knew the second he said it that he shouldn't have. He apologised.

The first black mark for a long time, did this mean he had lapsed? Was the Grey One back, was it her?

We returned home the day after Boxing Day to spend time with our other children and their families. He went to buy drinks as we were running out, and was very keen to go, I thought nothing of it, as he was always very helpful.

After half an hour I called him, his phone was engaged.

While he was in the bathroom before going to bed that night, I checked to see who he had spoken to on his phone while he was out buying drinks.

> *The Grey One was back! It isn't about physical signs. The atmosphere changes. There's a sense of unrest as that familiar unwelcome guest is back in the room.*

He had spoken to her for eight minutes while he was out buying drinks. It was very late, but I didn't care I phoned her number from his phone and left a very angry message.

He had been attending counselling regularly before Christmas, he had a break for two weeks over the holidays and he fell off the wagon! I was so very cross, hurt and disappointed that again while family were visiting he took the opportunity for betrayal.

He thought I would be too distracted with grandchildren to notice. I was never too distracted to notice.

I was not getting it. I see that now, I was as blind to the reality of our relationship as he was blind to the devastation he was causing.

January 2016 was exceptionally difficult, because she was back, her.

I could see in his eyes that I had lost him, what had been recovered for those few brief weeks were gone again. I felt as though it was me against the Grey One and her. Every time he went back after a break, her grip got stronger.

I was still definitely on his side but have no alliance with her. He was and still is my husband. She was and still is in an adulterous affair with him.

I was not ready to let him go. I wanted with all my strength to save our marriage. My fight was strong to rescue us from break up.

Photo Shopped

In our pastoral role we had heard so many people share the regret of walking away from their marriage due to adultery. I didn't want to be the one that gave up and walked away from ours.

Divorce divides a family, the couple heal and recover and make a new life for themselves. The children are the ones that are generally left with the guilt of which parent doesn't get to spend Christmas with them. The same despairing quandary repeats for every birthday, wedding day and the numerous other celebrations.

> *I vowed for better or worse, there are no guidelines in the vow to what goes beyond worse. If that place existed, I wasn't there yet.*

They are placed in the unenviable position as each year passes. As long as both parents are alive, having to decide which parent doesn't get to see them. The children are not at the altar when their parents say "I do", the vows were not theirs to make, neither were they theirs to break.

The broken promises and broken dreams are not their error, yet they pay the greatest and timeless price for the flaws of those who should be their strongest and most loyal bond.

I would have continued silently to pay the price for their father's secrets so my children were never put in the difficult dilemma of choosing between us, had he never have been exposed.

If the circumstances that split my family's future in two on that chilling Friday July 29, 2016, hadn't been discovered, I would still be his secret keeper.

Time to reflect ...

Should you be struggling with guilt over past choices and decisions, draw a line today. If you have to say sorry to anyone, say it. If you need to forgive someone, forgive him or her. This may include forgiving yourself. Don't allow the past to dictate your future. If you are alive and well, you deserve a happy and free life. Commit yourself now to a bright future, free from guilt.

Pray...

Heavenly Father, I pray on behalf of every broken relationship, whether they have, they might or never will repair. I lift broken people up to you in prayer now, I pray you will heal and comfort them as they step out of bed to live another day. I pray where children are involved you will cover them and protect them with your love and power.

Where divorce and remarriage are in their history, regretted or not, that you will bless and prosper present relationships. I ask where guilt exists you will remove it from their hearts and minds. Bad things happen that cannot be changed, but the vital need is for healthy hearts and relationships not to be hampered by their past. I pray you will redefine those who feel defined by mistakes and / or loss, to be free of guilt and shame and un-forgiveness of others and themselves.

Amen

1 Thessalonians 5:11

So speak encouraging words to one another. Build up hope so you'll all be together in this, no one left out, and no one left behind. I know you're already doing this; just keep on doing it.

(The Message)

Scene 12

Crimson Trajectory

The path that leads to demise is the only one you see,
You are looking, but believe it cannot be.
As you say – because it's not hurting me.

It was for this very reason, the children, I wrote to her following her recent unwelcome presence in my husband's life.

My husband is no longer available to you, I wrote,

You and he crossed a gross immoral line. You completely broke down trust in our marriage. You have had sex with my husband, on more than one occasion!! As long as you remain in contact, you will be a threat to our family! Please stop your involvement with him and let us recover. Now we have to start all over again because of your recent invasion into our lives.

A marriage and a family is a whole unit, you cannot secretly isolate yourself to one member of a marriage and family, it will always bring heartache when you do. In the history of mankind no one has ever had a freebie, payday always comes to the culpable in some form.

It destroys and steals loyalty and trust from within the marriage you tear apart.

He chose us – his family, this means he cannot have any part of the world you exist in anymore!

I hope this is my final contact with you. If tomorrow, in a few days, weeks, months or even years I find you have been in touch with my husband I will get in touch with a member of your family to gain their support in helping you to move on and put him behind you.

Their contact continued; I tracked her sister. I detailed who I was and that her sister was involved in an affair with my husband, and asked if I could rely on her to talk to her sister before more people were hurt by their behaviour.

All my interference did was strengthen their united force and cause me to feel more isolated within my marriage. My husband was angry at my meddling, he accused me of being vindictive, and it wasn't like me.

The tolerant one, blindly trusting in his word, had been the person he was used to me being. He was still attempting to convince me it was all her, that she wouldn't back off.

I was getting less and less tolerant. My goal posts were narrowing.

January 2016 was a horrid month!

The perpetual grim discoveries of the Grey One's deceptions were grievous.

I was soon to uncover the plans of a hotel room reservation in his diary. I let him know I had found out about this, he was annoyed. I don't know if the plans went ahead. The Grey One's onerousness at home was impenetrable.

We argued before he went to work as he had changed all his passwords and passcodes on his devices so that I could not access his calendar and emails etc.

Before slamming the door to leave for work his parting words resounded with a conviction of final resolve. "I want my life back," said the Grey One.

I was puzzled! What was the need in the Grey One's statement?

He provoked pains that were all too familiar with an injury he had not inflicted on me before. There was no attempt to mask his preference to continue his liaisons with her by the lack of remorse or assurance of an effort of change.

His unseen control was gone — the Grey One was exposed; there was nowhere to hide now.

I was overwrought with tears at his pretence of making progress in rebuilding our family; all that had been assembled was pseudo trust.

A wall built with bricks and no cement to secure them together will simply tumble down with the first blow. Trust is the cement that holds a relationship together.

I discovered a photograph on his mobile phone, I cannot describe the details of what I saw. It was sickening to the extreme. It was designed to incite indecency and lust.

I could not continue in this sadness. I needed a break. I packed a case and drove out of town for a few days to get some space where I could get some clarity in my head.

It felt liberating to be out of such a toxic environment. This was the most empowering action I had ever taken through my entire marriage. I sang my way along the motorway to the tracks on BBC Radio two. There were no tears! I think I would have had a breakdown had I not left that day.

I began to understand for the first time that I couldn't fight his addiction anymore, unless we were fighting together. Head to head conflict would never be the answer.

Reverend Grey

I was on the outside of my husband's life.

I had to get out of the way. It was too painful to carry on watching from the outside. I could not hold it together any longer. I was heading in a direction that was going to cause trouble for more people and more family breakdown. He was right, vindictive behaviour isn't like me.

At that moment I had no more resilience.

If our marriage could only continue by relying on my tolerance, it was all going to fall apart. I had to let it fail.

I tried everything to win his fidelity and loyalty and nothing had been successful. So I had to give him the space to make up his mind where his loyalties were.

Two days following my leaving home, I heard from him.

We met the following evening. We chatted generally over a coffee, I waited for him to begin, which he did, and he had learned his lines well over the years.

He was right that I needed things to be very different, which he understood. And knew what the big change needed to be; her.

The Grey One, as always, was grey in his response to change. He didn't want to say yes and he couldn't say no, he didn't want to see the light; neither did he want the dark. This is how he rolls, always grey.

He was fine in principle with my requests. Her? He would have to prove that to me over time.

We said our friendly goodbyes, I returned to my sisters, where I had fled to a few days earlier.

We had an important meeting in a couple of days; he needed me to be there. The day before the meeting he rang me, he gave me his word he would sort himself out.

I went home.

When I arrived we had a long heart to heart about the condition of our marriage. We were both defensive but at peace.

We went to bed, the reunion became intimate and all was well in those moments.

I determined my resolution.

He was attending counselling regularly and doing other things right. I conceded to allow him the

Of course he had no intention of making any changes — he needed me home.

time and space with his counsellor and others he confided in, to enable him to make the lifestyle changes necessary at the pace agreed by those he was accountable to.

I was willing and committed to giving him this chance. I wouldn't desert him yet.

If the Grey One ever gives me no other option but to leave him again, I would not come back a second time. I would not take that decision lightly. Having left once and felt the freedom of empowerment by doing so, I knew in my heart I could do it again. We could not continue without a step-by-step, day-to-day improvement.

The weeks rolled forward, sadness was my underlying mental and emotional state. This was not going to be an easy time for either of us. The Grey One was going forward with his addictive conduct and affair. By doing so it meant he was consistent in his deceitful pretences to his family and close friends. They were all sceptical. They were right to be.

My husband was looking at porn when he should have been looking at me.

He was sending intimate messages of love and desire to others, when his desire should be for me.

He was forsaking me, while keeping all others, when he should be forsaking all others and keeping himself for me.

Reverend Grey

Every vow my husband made on our wedding day, he practiced the complete opposite.

It seemed at times that most things were back to front in our relationship.

At our wedding he would have been more honest to make these vows:

> *Will you have this woman to be your lawful wedded wife?*
>
> *To live together against God's ordinance in unholy matrimony*
>
> *To dishonour her, mistreat her, and ignore her*
>
> *And forsaking her, keep thee unto another.*
>
> *I take thee to be my wedded wife,*
>
> *To have, but not to hold, from this day forward.*
>
> *I will dishonour you in the better times, and in the worst times,*
>
> *I will disrespect you when rich or poor,*
>
> *I will be disloyal to you in sickness, and in health.*
>
> *I will humiliate and abandon you,*
>
> *When we are parted by extra marital affairs.*
>
> *This is my solemn vow.*

These are the promises the Grey One has kept without exception.

Time to reflect …

I cannot advise anyone in similar circumstances. I gave my marriage every opportunity to survive without the agony of separation.

Our break up was inevitable, but I needed to be ready to accept it.

I chose to fake it until we make it – it wasn't the answer – I submitted to the torture of slow and painful torment.

I only hope this scene in our story brings clarity to someone who is walking a similar path.

Pray…

Heavenly Father, please care for the broken-hearted today, grant them the strength and resilience they need each day. Above all keep them safe in their pain, protect and shield their hearts and minds for future success.

Speak this Psalm out loud to yourself now, I have prayed in advance that it will comfort and strengthen you.

Psalm 91

> *You, who sit down in the High God's presence,*
> *Say this: "God, you're my refuge.*
> *   I trust in you and I'm safe!"*
> *His huge outstretched arms protect you –*
> * under them you're perfectly safe;*
> * his arms fend off all harm.*
> *Yes, because God's your refuge,*
> *He ordered his angels*
> *to guard you wherever you go.*
> *If you stumble, they'll catch you;*
> *their job is to keep you from falling.*

Reverend Grey

"If you'll hold on to me for dear life," says God;
"I'll get you out of any trouble.
I'll give you the best of care
If you'll only get to know and trust me.
Call me and I'll answer, be at your side in bad times;
I'll rescue you, and then throw you a party.
I'll give you a long life,
give you a long drink of salvation!"

(The Message)

Scene 13

The Grey Enigma

His conscience dimmed to almost black.
The day the light turns on – will mark the day
that he comes home.
Will we again become one? Are we intended to be?

Counselling continued with success to a degree, it was enlightening, but sadly not life changing. The counsellor confirmed so much of what I had assumed and more, and why I stood by my husband.

At the very first session the counsellor suggested that such was the depth of my husband's addiction and habitual sexual promiscuity, it would take a long and tough process to become completely free and whole. His commitment to the longevity of the programme would be crucial to success. He also shed light on the age of the persons the Grey One connected with on line as a clear sign that it was the unresolved Kenneth Theodore searching for unknown loss.

The counsellor went through my husband's life, finely dissecting every part. He made the connection between the events around his birth with events at seventeen. He also recognised the polarised compartmentalisation and disassociation disorder.

Reverend Grey

It was Easter 2016, the Wednesday before Good Friday, a hotel booking for 2pm that day popped into the Grey One's calendar, she had created the event.

The hotel was near where we live. I phoned him to tell him I knew what the plans were as I had seen them on his Google calendar.

He swore he had no idea how it got there.

I don't know if the liaison was called off or not, the invisible Grey One had become visible and it's my perception that this is not supposed to happen. She was moving the goalposts in her actions; she must have known I would see his calendar. What was the motive behind her decision to create an event in his calendar?

My husband had arranged to see his counsellor the same evening. I presumed he kept his arrangement, but the events that unfolded over the next two days made me doubt he had.

There was nothing specifically unusual about the evening. He didn't talk about the hotel booking or his meeting with his counsellor. It was Good Friday. I triggered a volatile switch.

I asked how counselling went two evenings ago. He wasn't at all keen to talk about it, he was defensive. I then reacted to his indifference with emotion, which escalated into a full blown torrent of anger displaying what I had become programmed to recognise as – if I put pressure on him he will silence me with his anger. Silent I was not, the separating option came up in the heat and emotion, which would only be said when the Grey One is personified in the moment of enmity between him, my husband and me.

I did not want a separation from my husband, but I did not want to live with the Grey One or her anymore. As much as I tried to make it happen I was not to have one without the other.

I backed off; we got up and got ready for the day. On the surface there was calm, inside I was churning.

Mid-morning my husband suggested we go for coffee at our local garden centre. This was a helpful move forward.

In the restaurant with our coffees he talked about his counselling session. I brought up separation and explained it was not what I wanted. He was surprised because he had offered me no promise of change.

We levelled again.

The Grey One had gone back into the shadows, he was out of sight until the next time.

I didn't make any more discoveries of the Grey One's plans for a few weeks.

We booked a holiday in the Canaries during the spring and had the best week's holiday I can remember for a long time. We didn't have one fall out, no arguments; neither did I sense anything suspicious.

Normally when we're on holiday the Grey One is eager to find Wi-Fi in a local café or bar and we would have to visit the same place every day so he could catch up on line.

It was usually a holiday habit to check emails and answer anything urgent. But not on this holiday. He didn't even take his phone or tablet out when we went for a walk or a meal. It was so refreshing to have a break from the anticipation of suspicion.

While we were relaxing in the apartment, I mentioned to my husband that I could live happily in a place like this abroad in our retirement.

We both got carried away with hopes and dreams of our future together, somewhere abroad but only a couple of hours flight back to England, we both began to dream about the possibilities.

Reverend Grey

I felt I could actually dream of a future without concern for the Grey One showing up. The holiday was coming to an end; it was the day to leave, we got packed and ready for the journey home.

We were watching the world go by in the departure lounge as we waited for our flight home. I went for a wander around the shops for a browse to kill some time. As I wandered back I saw him scrolling through his phone. Immediately my fears were triggered. I really wish I had not seen him on his phone, more so I wish he had not been tempted to look at his phone, but he did and I saw him.

It's fine. I guessed he was catching up on football results, it is Saturday. In an innocent attempt to calm my suspicious mind I approached him from behind so that I could see his screen.

A red mist came over me as I saw her face over and over again as he scrolled through the messages and photos she had sent him through the week of our holiday.

I was livid. I cannot fully describe in words how I felt in that moment. Sadly, to my discredit, I think everyone in the departure lounge soon knew he was having an affair. I was not quiet as I voiced my despair!

I had to cope in the only way I knew how to, so that I could sleep all the way home. I did sleep, truthfully I was unconscious, due consequence of my sedation methods.

I remember very little until the next day. We arrived home at around 3.30am; I woke up around 10am.

We had a quiet Sunday; the atmosphere wasn't great between us. The Grey One was annoyed with me for my uncontrolled display of emotion and too much alcohol which had caused me to vomit on the flight as well as being completely out of it.

He began browsing the Internet looking at one-bedroom flats. I couldn't cope that he was visiting the option of separation again.

With all the pain he had put me through, he punishes me for an emotional meltdown because of her invasive seductions and intent to ruin what was a very special and wonderful holiday. He could not see, or was willing to accept where the fault lay.

> *His pride is like a fortress built around the corpse of dry bones left in the wake of the beasts that have ravaged every ounce of his life from him.*

Did he really expect me to turn a blind eye while the duplicitous characters submit to Delilah's controlling manipulations under my nose?

This was too much.

How much more is he prepared to lose before he comes to his senses?

Time to reflect ...

You may want to think about this exercise my counsellor used in a breakthrough session with me during this term.

She brought Russian dolls and set them out on a table. I then had to name them. She gave me the names I needed to use for each doll then asked me to give the largest doll the name that had the strongest association in relation to my husband and me, and the smallest the weakest. It helped me to recognise how strong my loyalty is to my husband. I also saw where my loyalty needed to make a necessary change.

The largest doll was called 'Attachment', she sat close to my husband as the most important one in prime position. The next size down was called 'Fight' I placed her as close to my husband as Attachment as I had been fighting for my marriage all through our years together and had no intention to give up on that role ever. Doll number three was 'Loyal'. Yes she was up there beside the other two. She was the 'Secret Keeper'. The fourth was called 'Value', she couldn't sit too close as I felt little value in my marriage, she wasn't out of sight as I valued my marriage and my husband. Finally, the little one I named 'Flight'. She was off the radar, out of sight. I was never going to give up on my husband.

Scene 14

Equilibrium

Perverted addictions, a strong dark grip.
Her cause is every part to strip.
She will eat your flesh and chew your bones
Only the splinters will be spit.
Worth it all when out on the other side
When there is nothing more to take and nothing more to hide.

Kindness! This was my new coping strategy. I was done with the stress of conflict. It didn't help anyone. I was done with passivity, that didn't make any difference either. I had a new plan. I made up my mind from then I would kill my husband with kindness.

Meltdowns and hostility played into the Grey One's hands, as he found it easier to meet me head on with the offensive.

I know he found it very difficult to meet kindness with his offences. I could feel the tension to keep the Grey One in hiding while I was benevolent from my heart.

I also decided to be intentional in expressing my love and appreciation at least four times each day; when I woke up in the morning, before he left for work, when he arrived home from work, lastly before we went to sleep each night.

I meant every word when I said things like, he lights up my life when I see his face approaching me from the station when I pick him up in the evening. How it is my favourite time of day when he messages to say he is on his way home. That I was happy to wake up beside him every morning with a hug. I was grateful for his safe driving following a long journey. There were many more ways I could genuinely show my love and appreciation to him. I meant every word.

I intentionally began to hug him for longer, he would pull away after a couple of seconds, but I would pull him in for longer, I practiced this with purpose, to love our marriage back to health.

Everything within a marriage covenant that is so easily taken for granted, and it should be, I expressed my genuine love and appreciation for.

I embraced the next few months of our marriage; there were no arguments, no conflict or division between us.

It was the Reverend's birthday. I wanted to do something as a complete surprise for him. I love surprises, both giving them as I delight in watching someone receive a gift they do not expect and I love nothing more than getting a surprise too.

What I had planned for the Reverend was a night away in a hotel and dinner at a Thai restaurant. I checked in earlier in the day and took a change of clothes and toiletries for the Reverend. I set a bottle of champagne and glasses on the dresser with olives and nuts to snack on. I picked the Reverend up from the station then headed directly to the hotel without going home.

We enjoyed a fabulous evening together.

Weeks passed by, we were doing good I thought, getting on with the mundane, enjoying our usual routines and responsibilities, hugs, smiles and appreciation for each other.

Thursday July 28, 2016 was our date night, my stomach rolls when I think back to this date. The Reverend had been at work all day, a table was booked at an Indian restaurant we had visited before.

It was a wonderful evening, we chatted together as we ate our favourite food. We talked about our retirement, including the possibility of buying a property in Spain that we had discussed before. We laughed together too, silly things that no one else would find funny.

The night ended beautifully, this was the last time we were intimate with each other.

The next day was Friday – it began as usual. It was a beautiful sunny day and I dropped my husband off at the station at 6.15am, then as usual headed home and went back to bed with a cup of tea. I checked emails, filled in the daily recordings, which were part of my job every day.

> *As the lights went out on our date night for us to go to sleep, little did I know the lights also went out on my marriage of 34 years, 16 weeks and four days.*

I was meeting a friend for lunch at twelve midday so I went back to sleep with medication and set my alarm.

When I got up there was post on the mat, two or three letters.

Deep abandonment aroused from its sleep when I read the letter that had lay on the doormat for most of the morning.

The letter was addressed to my husband and her. In black ink on a white envelope were his name and her name, then our address.

What was I about to find out from this post?

There was not a doubt in my head that I should open it, I had no idea what to expect. I was not prepared for what I read.

I opened the letter; it was obvious that it was a business letter.

It read: Dear Mr Grey and Ms her, I am writing to confirm that your offer on a one bedroom flat has been accepted. The keys will be available for you to collect on Friday August 12, 2016, when you come into the office to sign the contract. Please bring with you your passports and a utility bill. You will both need to sign the contract.

It continued to address the financial expectations from them plus all other necessary details when renting a property.

> *I was on the outside of my life, looking on in disbelief as though in a terrible dream I wanted to wake up from.*

I was propelled into a tailspin, as an aeroplane rapidly descending to a spiralling crash landing. I was in denial to all the implications. I couldn't think past this moment. I felt as if nothing made sense.

In this nightmare I messaged my friend and apologised for letting her down and said that I would be in touch when I could.

I phoned my husband. He answered straight away. Without any small talk I began to read the letter to him. "Oh dear", was his response.

He was unable to talk as he was in an open office with others who would hear. He said he would phone me back in about twenty minutes.

I couldn't stay in the house, I had to drive away and find space and fresh air. I needed to be where no one could hear me talk or watch me deal with the elephant that came and sat on my chest.

I was seriously confused! I could not think properly, I felt empty of reason.

I waited forty-five minutes for him to call me. I messaged him and asked him to phone.

I was sitting on a bench situated on the edge of a lawn in a village square about five miles from where we lived.

He confirmed that he and her had been looking for a flat and that he was going to tell me next week that he was leaving me and they were moving in together and that he was sorry.

I wasn't angry, I was in utter shock. I was dumbfounded, but calm. He rang off saying we can talk later.

I immediately called a friend; there was no answer so I left a voicemail. I'm not sure how I was able to do this after all the years I have kept his secrets. I didn't rationalise it or weigh up the pros and cons, I simply left a message on a friend's mobile telling them the details of what had just happened.

I was only able to work out much later that had I not told someone immediately I might well have weakened with a few hours' notice and begged him not to go through with it. Which I believe is what he would have expected me to do, as it had been my reaction in the past.

A few weeks after our separation, I found myself regretting I had not found another way past the awful mess of the flat. Perhaps I should have put more space between the discovery and talking about it. I could have phoned the agent and said I was her and withdrew their names from interest, so that it wouldn't have gone through. Or I could have given him the opportunity to make things right. I had always rescued us from total wipe out in the past, why did it not cross my mind this time? I still cannot answer that.

I have spent years recovering from an emotional mess, making allowances, broadening the goal posts. This was the last time I would be at the direct mercy of my husband's infidelity.

I felt annoyed with myself for even thinking there was an alternative to separation. I would have always suspected there would be another flat, and if their relationship broke down, there would be another woman and the continuing battle against the awful websites.

> *I cannot remember all that he said that evening, except that he was intentional about moving out and the Grey One and her were going to live together.*

I picked him up as usual after work and we went to a local restaurant to talk things through. I was too volatile to talk at home, at least I would remain calm in public.

How could I respond to his unconscionable and unprincipled actions that have caused a maximum degree of pain to his children and me? Also to his excessive indulgence in casual and indiscriminate sexual relations?

Also, I could not continue with my career on my own. The role involved a deep emotional and selfless commitment to troubled young people. I am troubled and have been for years. With my husband beside me I could set my troubles aside as I had for my own children, but by myself I could not do this.

Neither could I continue with 'our life' without him in it, which would add greatly to my already immeasurable feelings of humiliation and loss.

I didn't want to live alone. It would be the worst possible situation for me.

I also knew, however, that I needed to burn bridges. For both of our sakes, I could not have a 'come back' for my husband to come back to. I would have him back in a heartbeat if I had remained in our home. My husband is my greatest weakness, my fondest love on earth and I knew he was making the biggest error of judgement of all he had ever made.

I cannot imagine never loving him, never feeling the bond of marriage union with him. My husband is a person who would not burn bridges. He would always keep his options open and always measure his bets. This is who he is – another shade of the Grey One!

It is my opinion, having known him longer than anyone, that he had no intention of telling me about the flat the following week. It was probably her intention that he did and he would have told her he would, because he must please her. He would have strung her along until such a time as we had a bust up, then he would have packed a bag and gone.

It was a surprise to me that I was so reconciled in my heart and mind; my decision to leave him first.

The letter, the flat, changed everything.

I love him still, but I realised I didn't need him as I had in the past. The previous year grew me in strength and independence.

I took control and with the conviction of steel I told my husband, if he was leaving on the twelfth then I would be gone by the tenth!

I would take to the road with my Yorkshire terrier and treat myself to a gap year! I planned to travel, visit family and friends for as long as it felt good to do so.

Family didn't need to invite me as I knew I was welcome to stay with all my children, sisters and parents whenever I needed to or wanted to, and for as long as I needed or wanted. Many friends had said the same.

I didn't want to put any time frames around my plans. I wanted to be free of responsibility, free to take opportunities that presented, and run with every possibility. I needed my life to look completely different from my life with my husband. I could not have anyone or anything demanding feed me, buy me, help me, take me, fetch me or wash me, clean me, mop me, vacuum me, dust me!

I only wanted to take care of myself and distraction would be my coping method.

I asked him to tell the children.

I also asked him to give the one month's notice required on our rented home and to contact the local authority to explain our role needed to come to a close as soon as possible.

These circumstances do not sound like we slipped into separation. It was calculated and planned for some weeks or months. I am guessing, based on knowing my husband, he went along with her agenda to please her. Sadly, she would have believed he was equally committed.

Three months to the day after I left that is how my husband explained "our folly" to me. That we "slipped" into a separation.

I put it to him that we did not "slip" into anything, it is impossible to equate flat hunting, followed by agreeing a contract with the time and effort that involves, and call it a "slip into".

He replied that he was swept along by the agenda and persuasion of another.

That is the Grey One, a chronic people pleaser, who runs with the moment, whatever the moment is at the time and whoever is of significance and influence in those moments. Of course he cannot say the word no! He must please. This time it was the Grey One and she, not my husband and me.

I spoke to my husband on the phone for half an hour; it was lovely to chat together.

How did I do it? How did I not feel anger towards him? His recollection of our separation had

> *He is a chronic people pleaser at the cost of his principles, values and his most precious loved ones.*

become somewhat grey around the edges. Not only was it his

opinion that we slipped into the way things are, but that I was resigned to the separation for a month before it happened.

How does he change the goal posts in the process of events to make the circumstances favour his position?

I was never resigned! That is a huge misrepresentation of my perspective. The Grey One said he was going to leave me and move in with her. That statement gave me no other option than to walk away from the toxic environment of the Grey One's painful intentions.

It frustrates me that he allows her to influence his mind now. He is not the world's greatest forward thinker; he just goes with the tide, always open to the power of suggestion, and I should know that as well as anyone. He doesn't make things happen, he allows things to happen.

Time to reflect ...

Though now in the present we are separated I believe he still loves me and misses me very much, as I do him. But his actions brought about circumstances that he couldn't control and those very actions, rescued me.

I believe that in my despair I fell into the master plan of my loving and perfect heavenly Father that day. I truly did not process a single thought regarding my personal outcome. My matter of fact announcement to leave first and be free of the noises was a script that had been written in the heavens. All I had to do was step into cast.

Pray...

Loving Heavenly Father, I pray for those who need a plan of rescue now, that you will write their lines and when the moment comes they will know exactly what to say and what to do.

Amen

Lyrics from *Above The Noise – McFly*

On the mystery of a love
That always finds itself in me
On the beauty of desire
That keeps calling me to deep
I've seen a lot of places
I've been to me and back
Every time I take that trip
I always over pack
I bring the dreams that charmed me
One's that owned my past
Why do I hold so tight the
Things that never last
I want a heart that hears you whisper

Equilibrium

I want these eyes to see your plans
I want a soul that holds to something
That's beyond these human hands
I want the feeling of your presence
I want to love to hear your voice
I want to live above the noise

Reverend Grey

Scene 15

Didn't I Say – Move Out Of The Way?

Resentment will rob you, so dump it.
Fear will freeze you, face it then walk through it.
A memory is sweet, remember it and cherish it.

While we were still under the same roof I wanted us to sleep together every night until our last. If we had separated there and then and taken separate beds, I would more than likely have got up in the middle of the night to join him. I could not hate him, it would have been impossible to hate him.

We talked about many things over the next eleven days. There were lots of tears and heart searching.

We attended church together for the last time, we were emotional. At the end of the service we held hands and prayed. I prayed that God would lead us both back to the cross where we could rediscover the one who could put us back together, whole and healed.

We went to a favourite pub restaurant for a roast dinner. He talked about how he felt that he is two different people. When he is with me, the other one doesn't exist, which is why he is convinced by his own lies. He believes the lie to be the truth one hundred per cent.

He said he would have found it so much easier if I had thrown him out of the house when I found out about the flat.

I knew it would, but I didn't want to throw him out.

I know him so well, he would much preferred to have left in a show down of anger and hostility, then I would have been the one left at home on my own to prepare to leave. He could only do this to me in anger. He would not have walked away while our love felt tangible. It would have been far more painful for me for him to leave me following an argument.

I had suffered more than enough. Travel, visits to family and friends for a year, would be perfect. I had lots of open invitations.

Throwing caution to the wind and shaking off responsibility of the mundane I will have myself a gap year!

I knew how I wanted our separation process to work out. I wanted to protect our love for each other and the transition and memory of it would be peaceful. As expected my husband agreed to everything I asked him for.

He confessed he was fed up of the lies and sneaking around behind my back and that he needed to get all his stuff and her out of his system.

We both knew our tears, though genuine and meaningful, would not halt the momentum that was gathering pace as the days passed by.

It was a beautiful sunny afternoon. We were sat at a wooden table in a small garden speaking of our love for each other. There was no offer on the part of my husband's or mine to change our plans.

I had underestimated how messed up he actually was. He had underestimated how much he was messed up too.

He regretted his decisions that brought us to that day, but that day was not the time to turn things around. He would not have maintained a change of mind for more than a day. We both agreed we would like to see each other from time to time. Not plan anything but randomly meet as and when.

My husband left for work at 6.15 the following morning. I dropped him off at the station, as had been our routine for many months.

My daughter was on holiday and I had no arrangements except to gain support from some much-needed friends and begin packing.

My friend listened to me speaking absolute gibberish, and nodded agreeably while encouraging me to be strong. Another was angry with the Grey One, and militant and unwavering in opinions of what I should and should not do. Wonderful friends.

The Grey One had begun the process of our separation! He had made the relevant calls.

I woke before 5am the next day. The words running through my head as I slowly came to were, "I will have nothing, but I will have everything."

I got it! I will have no home, no job, no responsibilities, but I will have far more than money could buy. I will have peace, freedom, no worries, no suspicion, no checking up or asking leading questions, no more lies. I will have my family and lots of friends and my faithful puppy. That is a lot of wonderful things to go forward with.

I suddenly became quite excited about my future, as though a weight of lead lifted from my mind. I am blessed and I am rich.

Wednesday, August 3 2016, I was leaving home number seventeen and my thirty-four-year marriage in a week!

My daughter and her family were coming home this day too.

The packing had commenced, I began with my clothes. This took a while.

Reverend Grey

Around lunchtime I messaged my daughter to see when she was getting home, we swapped a few texts then left it a while and carried on packing.

She messaged. "Are you ok?" …

"I'm just going to ask," she said, "has dad messed up?"

I rang the Grey One and explained our daughter's message and suggested we go to see her when I pick him up from the station. He agreed.

We arrived, they weren't expecting us.

Mum and I are separating, he offered. He took full responsibility for the reasons explaining he was moving into a one bedroom flat. There was a resigned response until her father said that he wouldn't be living alone, her and he were moving in together he told her. His darling daughter put her head in her hands and said, "Dad, that makes me very cross."

Emotionally, she asked if she was really worth it, probably not he replied with emotion.

Her father looked at me to answer their question of what brought him to his decision, I filled in the gaps. They were speechless!

They were supportive and understanding of my decision to travel. I got on with packing and was offered some available storage for a few months. I was grateful for that.

I am not usually self-absorbed, but this last year had been one big, fat drama. We needed to take our divided paths through the valley of doubts and climb back up to find a resolution for the damage that would bring closure to suspicions and deceptions. We needed to rediscover truth for ourselves in our own time.

There was not a single cross word between us the next weekend. We were not talking about the details of our situation so much. It was incredibly difficult for the Grey One to watch us separate our lives that was all down to his infidelity. I continued to show him love and kindness as I had done over recent weeks and months.

> *We both had to face our failings, travel through the tunnel of an uncertain outcome and come through the other side before we could fully know if our future would lead us back together or not.*

I was intentional about my attitude as knowing the Grey One as I did it would have made things far easier for him if I was hostile. I didn't want to be hostile at all during our final days together. I wanted them to be remembered as a peaceful and positive process.

It was two days before I left. Our home was beginning to look sparse.

The Grey One was taking Tuesday off, to help me with sorting out storage. We got into bed for a last night together; we hugged and kissed then fell asleep hugging each other.

The next morning he got out of bed after we shared a final hug. He came up to kiss me goodbye before he left. We kissed many times, how was I going to do life without this man, I thought to myself. Hardly a day had gone by without hugging, kissing and chatting, even laughing together. Since the invention of mobile phones, we would call, text and voicemail each other every day. He would phone me just to tell me how many times he had been to the loo in a day! Strange how what had been such a joy and avenue of communication for us had also turned out to be such a curse on our lives.

"See you later," he said as if attempting to say goodbye, but not forever. I totally missed his offer of a sensitive parting. "I will be gone before you get home," I replied, surprised at his remark. He explained his choice of words. That was probably the most planned comment he had made in months and it was lost on me, I'm not quick minded enough.

We agreed to see each other from time to time but not a regular arrangement.

I was expecting someone to come and fix the air conditioning on the car. It was going to be very hot, I needed air conditioning. I was very grateful for the use of his car.

The car mechanic arrived and got on with the job. I hadn't seen him before; he seemed a nice guy.

I still had plenty to do so I got on with it. Everything that was going in the car to take with me was beside the front door ready to load up.

The doorbell rang, the mechanic wanted our Internet password as he needed to find out about the problem with the air conditioner. He looked around seeing all the packing, and the room looking somewhat bare. "Are you moving?" he asked. "Yes," I answered. "Where to?" I explained very briefly, trying not to get into the real reason. He was much too chatty and I was telling him the whole sad story before I realised that I had said too much to rein it back in.

He was genuinely compassionate. He chatted to me for a little while, and then he put his arm around me, gave me and hug and a kiss on the top of my head and said, "You don't deserve to be treated like that!"

I didn't quite know what to say, I just smiled and said thank you. For some strange reason I was okay with the hug from a complete stranger, in my house, with no one else around. It was the first time I have ever had a kiss and a hug from a car mechanic!

When he had finished I asked him what the bill was as I had some cash. He refused to charge me anything and I could have this work done on him! How very kind and I got a hug and a kiss on my head too.

It took me until three o' clock to get ready for leaving. I was driving away from my home, my career and my marriage. I was moving away from being in close proximity to my daughter and her family and lots of close friends for the foreseeable future at least. My car was full with two large suitcases, one full of summer and autumn clothes, and the other full with winter clothes. I had no plan to settle anywhere any time soon so I needed to make sure I could survive for one year if I needed that long.

My pet and me set off for our unplanned adventure, with no clue where or when home would eventually be.

I was surprisingly excited.

Time to reflect ...

My faith in God is my first love and I trust him totally with my future. Faith grows stronger the more He proves His love and care with every detail of our lives. I know with a certainty He will never let me down.

Pray...

Heavenly Father, there are so many who do not yet know how much you love them. I pray through my story there will be opportunity for them to know you as I know you.

Amen

Psalm 23: A Psalm of David

God, my shepherd! I don't need a thing.
You have bedded me down in lush meadows;
you find me quiet pools to drink from.
True to your word, you let me catch my breath
and send me in the right direction.

Even when the way goes through
Death Valley, I'm not afraid
when you walk at my side.
You revive my drooping head;
my cup brims with blessing.

Your beauty and love chase after me
every day of my life.
I'm back home in the house of God
for the rest of my life.

(The Message)

Scene 16

Gap Year

Shipwrecked but safe to shore,
In for repair made ready to set sail one day.

My story is extreme, and I still only know that because of the expressions of shock on the faces of my family and friends as they hear me unveil another layer of the depth of addictive and promiscuous behaviour to which my husband descended.

I wasn't aware of how spoiled my mind had become. It was friends and family who recognised my inability to see how wrong things were, due to my blind loyalties towards Reverend Grey.

I will need help to unwrap the layers of impairment, and then to erase the stain and contamination my mind has been programmed to accept as normal. I will need to reboot my sensory receptors to achieve a correct perception and reasoning to what a marriage relationship should truly reflect if I am ever to be able to trust again.

I am who I am because of the unconventional fashion of my marriage. I now know that I can and will recover mentally and emotionally.

Over the years I have normalised my husband's addiction and become desensitised to the impact it has made.

I do not respond, as I ought, to the degree of the violence it caused.

My husband didn't master control in the early days to separate from the Grey One's influence when it came to seduce. It knew the Reverend's deepest and darkest want. It knew how to stroke his ego until he could not resist its lure. It did not stop enticing until it had stripped reputation, dignity and hope.

Then the fool was duped into paying the bill of consequence.

A high-end price tag of designer disbursement and the currency was his wife, family, many fond friends and two very successful careers.

I feel sad that for now my husband is completely dominated by the giant he is foolishly aligned with, and cannot say no to. I should feel humiliated and degraded, yet I feel I am rescued from the final outcome of a neglected sea vessel wrecked by a turbulent and raging storm. I was bailed out, overboard and I am safe, wounded but recovering, while my husband is stuck to the wreckage and is still going down with the ship.

To print our thirty-four year history is worth every word if it can prevent such extreme recklessness that exists to steal the soul from the core of other families.

Someone needs to break out of the silence and unmask the depravity that uncontrollable lust will crave!

My son and daughter met their father a while after we had separated. It was fourteen weeks after the separation, the Reverend had not seen his daughter since that day, and he missed his children and grandchildren so very much.

He appeared confused and upset. He said more than once, "I can't believe your mum left and we have sold all our things." She did what she had to do, they reacted. He said that if he had known I was moving out, he would have stayed in the house and I would have been able to come back when I needed to.

That was a confusing thing to say.

His son reminded his father that I left because he was moving in with her, that I was handed no alternative but to do so. Because I had forewarning through the estate agent's letter I was handed control of my own future, and was able to take my own plans forward.

Back Home

It was good to be back in the town I have called home for many years.

I had a few days with my daughter and her family, and then we were away together for ten days at the annual Festival, where a year previously Reverend Grey's morals had been exposed.

What a fabulous week it was back in the bubble of love, care and affection from many wonderful people.

Spiritually it was a remarkable time for me – but that is another story!

Someone once asked me what was the worst thing my husband had ever done? There are a few worst things that have affected me in different ways.

I couldn't say what they were. But they did involve her.

If you are wondering did they? The answer is yes, they did.

> *My marriage bed that was once consecrated, I felt was now desecrated.*

I hoped that we would be a positive example by the way we handled the shameful and humiliating exposure. As a whole family we would stand united to defeat the assailant of my husband's public demise.

We still can, it's not too late for my husband to defeat the Grey One so that he disappears to nonexistence.

The family and I are rebuilding our lives together, estranged from him for now.

This will not be the end of my story, however! I am on an assault against everything that facilitates deception and betrayal within an intimate relationship such as marriage.

I know that deceit and betrayal go hand in hand with humanity, affairs will continue, relationships will end, pain won't stop. My argument is with those who both encourage and facilitate betrayals and deception through the secrecy of the Internet.

During the first few months of my 'gap year' I had a wonderful and difficult time.

I travelled from town to city to villages in the Midlands, the Cotswolds, Wales, South West, South East and Northern Ireland. I have visited family and friends, had the privilege of sleeping in some lovely, warm, cosy and beautiful guest rooms and eating fabulous food.

I decided it was time to open my laptop and begin to follow up some administration. I had responded to messages on my phone, but I hadn't felt motivated to catch up on the more mundane tasks.

What stared me back in the face from the screen was a shock I never expected.

How could he? The Grey One shook my world once more. Yet again he extravagantly cashed a non-returnable cheque from my overdrawn emotional and mental bank account!

What I discovered took my breath away! How many more ground breaking tremors are going to fracture my stability? When will the Grey One be done for good?

It was so careless of him not to shut his email account down. I can take a look anytime through the square screen on my lap, to see written in black and white the Grey One's adulterous lifestyle.

The details of his betrayals left me sick in my stomach. To see emotional and financial investment in her was cruel. Must he please her to the degree of agony to his family and me?

He is so morally corrupt with no concept of the depth of degradation he has blindly succumbed to that he believes his life is manageable.

He is clean and shaved; he smiles in the right places and is funny at times. His flat will be spotless, tidy and well managed with no one to answer to – yet! Until the day his conscience invades his lonely-heart's door and penetrates through the lies he mistook for truth, the darkness he mistook for light and the lecherousness he mistook for love.

It is my prayer that pure love will devise a way and the means to cast warmth that will draw him like a moth to a flame, to melt the icy precipitation of his own cold demise so it will drain from his feet.

Time to reflect ...

The sponsored talk-a-thon had begun, this was how I coped. I was able to go over and over again the details of my tragic real life drama, with the lovely family and friends I spent time with. Every time I arrived at a different home I took a deep breath and relished the opportunity of going over it all again. I had to talk it out, in detail, over and over again. I would have been far too consuming and self-absorbed to stay with one person or family for too long at a time. I was most incredibly blessed to have as many supporters as I have, sponsoring me in kind and time. I needed that. It is the virtue and quality of the family I married into and the organisation we worked for, that resulted in my gathering such a wonderful bunch of friends and the support they are to me. And they would have been there equally for my husband had he bailed out of the sinking ship with me.

I cannot stress enough the need to talk, it is a most healing process, and it releases tension and anxiety.

What I couldn't handle was small talk or trivia, this frustrated me.

If I can give any advice it would be to not overburden one person, it can burn people out and spoil friendships. Share the load, so that many carry a small part of you at a time.

Pray...

Father, reveal those who can share our troubles with us and in the process make those friendships stronger. Help us to be aware of their needs too. Above all thank you that we can lean into you with the whole lot of it and we will never be too much for you.

Amen

Psalm 34:17, 18

*Is anyone crying for help? God is listening,
ready to rescue you.*

*If your heart is broken, you'll find God right there;
if you're kicked in the gut, he'll help you catch your breath.*

(The Message)

Reverend Grey

Part 3

Wake Up!

It's ok to hit the rock.
The most important thing is to believe you can mend,
then climb back up, to fight for your dreams.

It took him a full month to move out of our home after I left. He took what he needed for the flat, gave some things away, the rest got sold or went to the tip.

The bed I bought for our thirtieth wedding anniversary got sold for a measly seventy pounds. That was more than its value to me, it only reminded me of the Grey One's lack of dignity.

The Grey One eventually moved into his flat.

In those early weeks of separation I was somewhat driven to talk rapidly, and erratically. Though my mind was steady and my outlook was positive, stress and anxiety to my nervous system was evident. It may not have shown too much on the outside as I am far too well practiced at keeping a cool exterior.

I met my husband. This was the first time I had seen him since I left him.

He was first to arrive.

As I walked around the corner, I saw him immediately, and he saw me, but he acted as if he hadn't. He was scrolling through his phone as if he was far too interested in it to be thinking about me. This was another of his weird practices. Pretending he hadn't seen me if we were meeting somewhere. He would appear interested in what may be happening in the opposite direction, until I was right beside him. It always felt as though he could not appear to be looking for me, or watching me as I approached him.

Was that because he didn't want to look as though he was depending on me in some way or waiting for me to arrive? Or again was it guilt and shame that would swell in his conscience at the sight of me? Then he would look with an air of surprise on his face when I came up close.

He did look genuinely pleased to see me, even though he acted startled.

We hugged, he kissed my cheek, and he bought drinks. We chatted generally at first.

She still hadn't moved in with him. He welled up several times through our conversation.

Sadly, now it was not so simple for him to walk away. He was stranded in the invisible world he had created yet continually denied existed. What he failed to include in this fantasy world was a get out clause. But of course we know that doesn't come with the package, there are no exit signs or return slips.

He must first want to rediscover his faith, then his honesty, loyalty and integrity, and be very brave. Only then, will there be a way back.

I bear no malice towards my husband. How could I? He is troubled enough and I love and care for him very much. I hope he finds help to get back from his mess. He will need to dig deep to find the strength to get free from the muddle he has got himself into, to bring order back to his life, instead of confusion and chaos.

We both need to find our own way into a correct state of good mental and emotional health. We cannot do this together, I see that more clearly now. We have, for too long, enabled each other to disappear further into a degraded psychological mental state. This characterised how we responded to each other's actions and reactions, and would continue to do so if we were still together. We both agreed that if we do discover a way to continue with our marriage, it would take a long road to get us there.

We hugged tightly before we parted, he cried, I cried. He later told me he sat weeping in his car for half an hour before he could drive away.

He wrote to me saying...

I am desperately sorry for the way I have treated you and would give anything to change the past. Sadly, it is what it is and the very public exposure of my failures and subsequent behaviour makes it impossible for me to come back to what was. I think that would make our lives more difficult and stressful and you would never be free of the suspicion and mistrust that have hounded our lives. I think you are better free of me and despite how you feel now will have the opportunity to build a new, happier life.

I often think of you and the wonderful life we had together with much love, but also a desire that things could have been different. But wishful thinking never got me anywhere as you well know. I miss you terribly at times and it is painful writing this but I don't miss the hurt I continually caused you by my behaviour. I really feel you are better off without me and will gain much help and support if I'm not there.

Love you always, miss our dreams, miss you, miss the relationship I had with our children. Miss the certainty of growing old together and feel incredibly sad that I mucked up so badly in every way and that we have no home; no future and I have no promises I can make.

I went to visit a lovely lady. While we were talking about how difficult life has been, she made reference to an email she had sent my husband three years prior to his exposure. She expected me to know about it, I had no idea she had sent an email that would relate to his current circumstances.

> *It's never too late to rebuild and restore, he will see that one day I believe.*

I asked her to forward it to me, which she did.

I have to include this in my writings, as other Christians need to know what happened. Anyone who takes his or her Christian faith seriously will want to read this and fully absorb it.

This is what she sent me. I have removed names and any other references that may be recognised.

She wrote to my husband, the Reverend, he was her minister at the time. It read,

> *Hi, I have had a couple of disturbing dreams; I am certain they mean something when they won't leave me! In my dream my husband and I were out having a meal somewhere, I noticed he had fallen asleep. I threw something at him to get his attention. When this didn't work I got up and went to him. When I got to him, I realised he was dead!*

> *As you can imagine I was really shaken by this dream so I asked a Christian friend to interpret it for me. I have known her for many years and trust her interpretations.*

> *This is what she wrote back:*

I don't think your husband is your husband in the dream, but rather your husband is representing your pastor, and you are representing his wife, who because of secret sin/lies to the church and God is 'falling asleep'?

(*In the Bible it says that anyone who takes communion (the bread and wine) irreverently is like a person who jeered and spat on Jesus at His death. We have to examine our motives and test our hearts and eat and drink in holy awe.

If we give no thought (or worse, don't care) about the broken body of Jesus when we eat and drink, we run the risk of serious consequences. That's why so many of us even now are weak and sick, and others have gone to an early grave. If we get this right now, we won't have to be sorted out later on. Better to be confronted by the Lord now than to face a fiery confrontation later.)

The dream interpreter went on to say,

Anyone living in a deliberate rebellious condition prior to communion and intends to continue in that state afterwards is running the risk of serious consequences should they partake of the bread and wine. The outcome of running this risk is described as a slow motion, gradual death.

When a believer is living wilfully against God's word in defiance to Him and intends to carry on after taking communion, he or she is engaging in a public lie and must face the consequences of their blasphemy and for undermining the integrity and reputation of the Christian body that are the church. You were given this dream so action can be taken before the person falls asleep.

Reverend Grey

I can believe why the Reverend, as he was then, ignored this. What was even more accurate about this dream is the woman who had the dream and her husband who was asleep in the dream, had the very same names that my husband and her used on line.

By this time though my husband was far too deep in his mess to be able to walk away and stay away, he knew it too. He was in free fall. I guess he would have put this right out of his mind, continuing on regardless. In the past my husband has always landed on his feet. If not he would wait, face the consequences, suck it up and deal with them, and then land back on his feet.

It is a common default that Christian leaders will put the spiritual and emotional welfare of the people they are responsible for before their own. Then, without thought put others' needs before their own or their families.

Most of us have travelled on an aeroplane. As part of the presentation we are taught every time we fly of the procedures in an emergency. We are told to make sure we have our own life jacket and mask on before helping anyone else with theirs. Even before our own child.

A parent that refuses to cut corners and break rules, protecting themselves first from harm before protecting their children does not make them a perfect parent – but it does make them a safe parent.

The perfect leader, Reverend, coach or parent will never exist. But it is their responsibility to be a safe one.

This is a powerful parallel of the importance of keeping our own hearts and mind in safe mode from the temptations that will sabotage our soul the moment we step out of the front door.

Someone needs counsel, someone else is sick, a marriage is in crisis and a teenager has run away from home. Just a regular day for a Reverend. Don't cut corners on the protection of your soul like the Reverend did.

*1 Corinthians 11: 27-30 The Message

Here are other scriptures where people have lied to God and His people and have died: Joshua 6:7, 2 Sam.6. John 10: 28&29, John 15: 2-6, 1 John 5: 16&17, James 5:20, 1 Corinth: 3:15, 1 Corinthians: 5:5, 2 Corinthians: 2:5-8, Acts 5: 1-11, Ephesians 2: 8&9

Time to reflect ...

If you are in Christian leadership, I cannot encourage you enough to fully examine your heart and absorb Paul's strong encouragement to live every day in repentance and His forgiveness. The only way to prevent an outcome similar to my husband's is to invest daily in your own personal relationship with God, keeping your heart washed and your hands clean. Narrow your grey area; it is a playground for your enemy to plant traps for you to walk into and bombs that will blow up in your face when triggered.

Pray now, put the book down and talk to your Heavenly Father... right now!

Psalm 24

Who can climb Mount God?
Who can scale the holy north-face?
Only the clean-handed,
 only the pure-hearted;
Men who won't cheat,
 women who won't seduce.

God is at their side;
 with God's help they make it.

(The Message)

Prodigal Husband

The pigpen is repugnant.
When others tell you of its offence,
You deny it – you cannot smell it
For it is the place that you inhabit.

What can I say? This meeting and the account of the dream that had been shared with the Reverend made me feel very sad, because I wanted to shout at him, shake him violently to save his life so he would begin to put things right and thrive again.

The talk-a-thon continued. I still had no desire to live alone and neither could I contemplate the thought process of considering any options.

Then came an unexpected surprise, my daughter-in-law asked if I would like to live with them. Their unexpected level of generosity shocked me.

I would be living in a town I hadn't lived in or worked in before, so I could make new memories. There would be no history to claim ownership of my mind, which is more than helpful for the benefit of moving forward.

The sight of settling down and having a home again was welcome. The transient life I lived with my husband and family led us to move house regularly, this would be my eighteenth home in thirty-four and a half years.

I met my husband for the second time since we separated. We had breakfast together.

He shed tears again for his loss and for the grief he had caused. He had met our eldest son a couple of days before and was due to meet our youngest son the following week. He says the same to all of us, he talks of his regrets and loss, shame and guilt, yet does nothing to put them right.

He repeated a phrase to me that his son asked of him, which was "show us you're changing", words of change are hard to take if they are not followed with action. All we see is that he is making it more difficult to remove himself from his situation.

> *He is a hard nut to crack — even for Almighty God!*

We parted with tears and hugs. His closing words were "I will do something soon, I promise."

Over a period of weeks my husband wrote me some lovely emails, how he missed me and loves me and how he cries when he thinks of me.

He wrote to me again following a message I sent him. He said,

> *Like most of your messages they make me emotional and tearful at what we have lost at the moment, never mind the broken family connection.*
>
> *You ask a lot of questions that I don't answer as the answer is not cut and dried, and the underlying reason for that is the problem that caused so much of our turmoil through marriage, our exit from our career, which we both loved, and our separation, is still with me.*
>
> *It's not your fault, you are beautiful and lovely and deserve far more than I gave you. It is a weakness/addiction in me. And above all else I am trying to be honest with you and myself for the first time, as hurtful as it is for both of us.*
>
> *I will always love you and will always seek to do what is right for you. I cry when I think of you*

without me. I miss you terribly at times including sexually and if this were written on paper it would be soggy with my tears.

But to start a journey back together without honesty or me being on the road to recovery from this addiction would drive me back into the secret life I am finally breaking free from.

Love you xxx

A friend of mine asked me to house sit for a weekend, which I was more than happy to do. Surprisingly it was a difficult few days, but the housesitting was not the problem. It was meeting my husband the previous day. I am always upset for a day or so afterwards.

When my friend arrived home, we sat and had a long talk; she was very helpful to me in a very personal way. How much we need our friends, my friends have been lifesavers!

I gave my husband his presents when we met for Christmas shopping for the family. He was surprised yet happy to have them and save them for Christmas Day.

I had spent all morning preparing my head to be kind with a good attitude while I was with him. I failed miserably!

Within ten minutes I had vented all my frustrations and anger towards him, detailing his long list of offences against his family and me. The need was deep within me to accuse him, accuse more, and continue to accuse him, to compensate for the years of excusing him. This is a process I need to seriously address in the not too distant future. I have seen the consequences of storing up bitter offences in many others,

> *I want to keep a short account of forgiveness, as the alternative is bitterness.*

enough to be warned that its unhealed symptoms are self-destructive.

It didn't take long before he was angry with me. I regretted later that I had forced his anger, I didn't do that again.

We went for lunch – the atmosphere became calmer. He opened up about his hopes to see his family over Christmas, and how much he misses them.

Again, as when we had met twice before, he cried and confessed the mess he had got himself into and that he was stupid to pay for a trip to Paris for him and her, which was the financial investment that affected me so horribly when I opened my laptop a few months earlier, and even more stupid for allowing her to move in with him. He admitted he regretted getting involved in destructive sites and wouldn't wish his situation on his worst enemy.

He knows she is the only reason his children won't accept him as part of the family at the moment, the children would never contemplate her inclusion in their lives due to the damage she played a large part in to cause. She was equal to my husband in the lies, deceit and betrayals that her family know little or nothing of.

I struggled even more after seeing him on that occasion as all his tears and regrets disappear once I am out of sight. I messaged him twice following our time together with strong words of frustration and fondness in an attempt to keep alive the part of my husband that had been very much still responding to me when we were together. Sadly he had disappeared into his other self within hours of our parting.

I have been insulted in the most humiliating way possible, but I don't feel it, I don't know how too.

I have been neglected and left with nothing, no home and no security, I don't feel that either, I don't know how to.

Financial emotional investment that should have been banked with me has been banked with others, while I have been left overdrawn on. I don't feel that either, I don't know how.

I need to feel, so that I can heal. I have become so good at looking and speaking as though everything is fine, when it is very seriously not fine.

I don't know how to properly connect with how very bad things were and still are, and feel the appropriate emotions that I should feel.

I left my new hometown to meet my husband at 10am the morning before I was moving into my new home with my son and his family.

He loaded all my belongings that had been in store into a van, for which he paid the hire fee. (My son-in-law generously drove it to my new home for me the next day and helped me move.) I got a Christmas present, very nicely gift-wrapped, he kissed me three times on the lips in quick succession, and said, "I love you loads," then walked away. I watched him go. I tooted my horn, as I wanted to give him eye contact just once more. I smiled and waved, he smiled and waved back.

I moved into our lovely new house, I am very happy with how my life is shaping up.

A week later it was Christmas. Wonderful, I was ready.

My husband left an emotional message on Christmas morning. He spoke to each of his children too, fondly wishing them all a happy Christmas, and he sounded sad they all commented. I called him back later; he was chirpy, drizzling maple syrup on his parsnips. That annoyed me, that he sounded chirpy. Honestly…I prefer to hear him sad. He would have missed us all desperately I'm sure.

Christmas 2016 was one like never before, as usual it was good chaotic. Continual rotations of eat, clear up, drink, and clear up, lots of noise, laughter and chatter. We were a crowd; all pitching in together, the children were very happy and excited.

There was no Grey One to manage, or to worry myself with thoughts and fears of when he would disappear into the Grey, in the basement of his life.

That is his home now – the basement.

To be expected I had a few low days following the Christmas holidays. I was on my own and feeling sad. I re-centred my focus, I was honest about my feelings for my husband. I arranged to see him, I wanted to tell him face to face that I couldn't give up on him – the bond is too strong. I hadn't disqualified him, neither had the children, he had disqualified himself and it was his call as to when he reverses his choices. We are all still here, at the moment, waiting for his return.

He sobbed like I have never known him sob before about how he had betrayed me. He could not believe that I was sitting with him, still loving him and forgiving him. He wasn't telling me anything I didn't know, things that he was forgiven of already. I get him, no one knows him like I know him. I have lived with him longer than anyone else in his life and longer than anyone who is ever likely to. His children come second, third and fourth in line after me, but they don't get him like I do. I am the only one who knows the whole person of who he is; the good, which is very good, the bad, which is very bad and the ugly, which is very ugly. Not forgetting how very funny he can be, especially in front of a crowd.

He sobs, yet doesn't realise that in his current situation he is still storing up more regrets, and what he is doing now is much worse than anything he has done in the past, because he has allowed himself to completely abandon his moral responsibility to his family.

In a pub, sobbing with remorse about deeds committed twenty-five or more years ago, then to leave me, to go back to committing more offences against his family and me, is unfathomable.

When will he sob for what he is doing now?

I knew from Tuesday August 25, 2015, that he would have to get much worse before he could begin to get better. I remember saying to my daughter at the time that we may have to lose dad to his dark world for a season. It's my hope he will recover and become completely whole someday.

Her, who he is involved with, won't even scratch the surface of knowing him, she never will. She will never know him as a whole person, she will never know or see him as a father, or a grandfather. She will never know the talented, outstanding, inspiring, funny leader, who saw potential in the most unlikely people, who he fathered, nurtured and equipped to become their very best, even better that he will ever be.

She will never see him captivate a congregation with encouraging and challenging teaching that will never be forgotten.

When a person bewitches someone precious from the core of a family he loves, they can never capture the core value of them. They can only have the weak damaged shell, and then whatever they invest into them will be like putting money into a pocket with holes in it. The true virtue or essence of them cannot be lost.

Imagine a very precious and extremely valuable jewel that has been passed on through countless generations and future generations are waiting to own this wonderful gift that has been given to one deeply loved in an age long past. It stares back at every member of the family with all the love and warm memories of the times it has been worn by parents and grandparents. It carries fondness and attachments of their romantic history.

If a thief stole that precious jewel from the family, it would only be for what they could selfishly gain from selling it. It could offer them nothing more.

Pornography selfishly steals from others for egocentric gain with little regard for others. Whether it is a picture, a video, sex text or sex call or ultimately fulfilling pornographic behaviour physically with someone who belongs to someone else and another family, it can never be anything more.

The peace and freedom and joy of family life, or a pure wholesome life with my husband, can never be hers. We had and still have the best of him.

Who she has is the mental disorders and the symptoms of them. She has the brokenness and his need to satisfy his people-pleasing side effect, both practically and lustfully. Yes, he will please her, but that is his need, to fill the void he has never given anyone a chance with, since his continual attempts and disappointments as an infant.

She is only compatible with the Grey One; she has nothing in common with my husband. He can never be two identities at the same time again. Those days are over.

The Grey One is not hidden and unseen in the shadows now, to be packed in a bag to come out and change into when he is out alone and away from home and family and friends.

My contact with my husband is limited while he is the Grey One; while he is living a life his family cannot be part of. His children cannot visit his home; he cannot talk about his personal life while his life revolves around her and all she represents.

It is too upsetting and hugely frustrating that he is so lost and out of reach. No one will have the best of what years remain for him to live until he faces up to his damaged mind and emotions then comes back home to his real life and his faith and family.

He has tried and failed more times than can be counted to find a way through the misty maze of incoherent and undistinguished conflict of opinion, actions and character that has no logic, reason or fluency. The essence of his confusion is deep and delicate, protected by his self-made flesh of tender soft tissue, covered by an exterior that appears resilient and strong but is not desensitised from the pain of the biological process it will take to penetrate. He will need to be prepared to brace, to break the neck of the broken and impaired replica of himself to eventually find the original person he was born to be.

I believe I recognise her plot all along – why she continually posted sexualised photographs and messages to his phone while he was with me, appealing to his desire to submit to her pleasures to please her, and his inability to say no when she told him of her need for him. To use the

I drove home with a massive grin on my face, I have no idea why. I felt as though heaven was smiling on me.

alternative ploy and obsess about his needs of her and what he wants her to do for him would not have aroused him quite so much. In all the evidence I have of their entanglements, it was her role to need and his need to please.

She was so threatened by our marriage that she feared losing what she had of him to me. She mastered the plans alongside her persuasive enticements knowing he would not resist her.

The Grey One does not have the Reverend or me to retreat to anymore. She has the noose around his neck and the hook through his nose. He says he cannot get himself out of his mess. He has admitted as much to some he has spoken to. He recognises the mess, but does not want to face the pain from the noose or the hook if he attempted to break free! One or the other or both, they will be painful to extract from.

I handed the timing of his initial exposure into the hands of his heavenly father and his family, now I hand over the timing when he will have the courage to return like the Prodigal back into the arms of God and his family.

He, Almighty God, is the one she needs to be in fear of. *"It is a dreadful thing to fall into the hands of an angry God." *"For God is not an indifferent bystander, He is actively cleaning the house and He won't quit until it's all clean". *"For our God is a consuming fire".

> *Be brave my love, you can walk away.*
> *Don't wait for the fire, literal or figurative, to once*
> *again intervene in the life of the one... 'Born of Fire'.*

Time to reflect …

All I can say here is if you are in the pigpen – get up and go home.

Go as you are into the heart of those who love you. They are more than likely watching and waiting for you to return. Just as we are looking out every day for my husband to come home.

Pray…

Father, walk with those the mile it will take to go home and never leave their side.

Amen

Luke 15:19-24

He got right up and went home to his father.

When he was still a long way off, his father saw him. His heart pounding, he ran out, embraced him, and kissed him. The son started his speech: 'Father, I've sinned against God, I've sinned before you; I don't deserve to be called your son ever again.'

But the father wasn't listening. He was calling to the servants, 'Quick. Bring a clean set of clothes and dress him. Put the family ring on his finger and sandals on his feet. Then get a grain-fed heifer and roast it. We're going to feast! We're going to have a wonderful time! My son is here – given up for dead and now alive! Given up for lost and now found!' And they began to have a wonderful time.

(The Message)

*Hebrews 12:28&29 – Read this in correct context within the passage it is written. Fire burns the rubbish but precious stones and metal will not burn. Those with pure motives and a clean conscience will be preserved. *Hebrews 10:31 – Again read it in correct context within the passage it is taken from. God's anger is often taken out of context. He grants humanity our free will and will not take it away which results in many tragic outcomes. God's anger burns against those who wilfully violate the defenceless, and cause pain and death.

Reverend Grey

To The Precious Emerald...

The truths now unfold, the story has been told
No more crying eyes, no more hidden lies.

*A*u *Revoir* my Handsome, Born of Fire, Gift of God,

I look forward to the day I will see you again, the original masterpiece of who you are I mean. The one I fell hopelessly head over heels in love with. Neither of us can know when that will be. I know I will love you, but you will be a different person, I will be different too.

There is still a strong part of me that believes we will grow old together, should we live long enough. I need to give God and time an opportunity to redefine us.

That August, I cleared everything that was mine out of our thirty-four years, then left. After I had gone, it was your turn to clear out the rest, to keep what you wanted and needed, and then you cleaned all through. You swept away the dust and dirt that had gathered because of neglect. You washed the windows and bleached the bathroom and kitchen and mopped the floors, pulled out weeds as you tended the garden. I know you would have done a thorough job before you left for good, never to return. The only room left to make clean is the basement.

> *Physically, I am free now. I can go where I want to without fear. Except for the basement, I won't go there ever again.*

If I meet you there, I shame you, because it's so dirty and I reflect your guilt, which makes

231

you cry and that makes me sad, then it makes me even more sad to watch you return to the basement when you walk away.

You are free to live the life you have kept secret for so long, in the basement. Free to do what you want to do, with whom you want to do it. It's not a secret place anymore! You can come and go as you wish. Your family cannot visit you there though. They cannot be part of the cellar you now call home. Occasionally you can pop out to see them, but it's awkward, because you are dressed in your dungeon clothes, which are stained with the scandals of the cellar. The odour permeates and contaminates conversations and activities. You try hard to hide the stench, but it's impossible.

The very place I have worked so hard to keep you out of for years, is where you live for now. You are searching for life in a grave among the dead.

It's time for the most difficult part of our separation and it will take a while.

I need to roll back the rug of secrets and clear out all its lies, item by item. I need to lay it out so that I can see it all for what it is. Consider it, then address it, whatever that may mean for each piece. Nothing must be kept, it all must go. Then I will be pure again, decontaminated from all the sins – spiritually, emotionally, physically and sexually.

The basement is your business, not mine, for you to sort out, not me. I will leave you to it.

Then my love it will be your turn, in your time. The basement is all yours. Life above the basement with your family is slippery for now until you come back through the trap door, never to return, to live a moral, integral and honest life with your family and others who love you. Living a life your family can be proud of.

To The Precious Emerald

We are all waiting for you to clear out your closet, then come back, however that will look when it happens.

I left you for our good, not to add to our demise. I don't feel sad or angry with you.

I am different, I have surprised even myself. Time has passed since we separated and I am coping. I am enjoying a freedom I haven't been able to appreciate for a very long time. The possibilities are limitless and I will embrace them all. Nothing is holding me back; I don't need to guard the trap door to the basement. I'm not confined to the rug that keeps the pile of secrets hidden from family and friends. Neither am I there to make you angry by bringing the Grey One into the light.

I guess we both need time to figure out our individual process. I cannot tell you how to work your stuff out, while I don't know how to work my own stuff out. My energy will be better spent where I can make positive changes for the better, which is on my own issues and flaws.

For us to grow old together, not only do you need to be a changed man for me, I need to be a changed woman for you. It never has been my responsibility to run your life, or cover for you; I regret that I did that. If I had learned these things years ago, we may already have been through this process and survived with far less harrowing consequences. You are my husband, I am your wife, but I resign now from the self-promoted role of managing director of your life.

I was wrong to keep your secrets. I was wrong to enable you to live a double life for as long as I did. I should have spoken.

It isn't too late.

When you eventually find the will and have a mind and strength to master the Grey One, you can be restored and still do great things – like Moses, David and Paul, they failed, made mistakes, committed sins yet God still used them.

Reverend Grey

Remember tomorrow is a clean sheet of paper; It has no mistakes on it yet.*

In that tomorrow, you will find my door is open. It was never even shut.

With all my love as ever and for always.

Your wife

x

* *Anne of Green Gables: L M Montgomery*

To the Future Me...

Don't look back, only forward. Yesterday happened, you cannot change it.

Be prepared for what is in store.

Your life will expand; I am not through with you yet. The pieces of your life are being put back together to be made into something better than ever before.

The rest of your life will be secure, unspoiled by the sins of others, you will more than survive.

A new chapter is being written, and the script is changing direction. You are in good hands.

You will see him, it may take a year, and it may take five years, or more, before he returns. You have that time to live, time doesn't stand still for anyone; there is no pause button. You won't get a second chance to live these months and years again, so be ready to embrace them and live them to their fullest. Imagine what can happen in the next ten years, you probably haven't imagined big enough.

> *Because I will know him; the Handsome One, Born of Fire, and Gift of God.*

Every day, wake up in the morning, and think what a precious privilege it is to be alive, then count your many blessings.

From yesterday's you...

Only God knows who and where I will be, when my prodigal husband returns to the way of the cross. One thing is certain, when he does, I will recognise him immediately...

Time to reflect ...

If you have made it to the end of this book I want to say thank you for your time and commitment to a difficult read.

You may not know God as your Heavenly Father or be a follower of Jesus, maybe you know God and your faith has lapsed for reasons that do not matter now.

I could not end without asking you to consider stepping into the wonderful life God, your creator, offers you.

If you have looked at the church in the past as an example of Christlikeness, you may have felt disillusioned by what you have seen.

I'm sorry for that, the problem is we are all deeply flawed and far from perfect. But what we do have is a loving and forgiving Father who never runs out of patience with His children, and He wants you to be His child too, to share in His inheritance from now until eternity.

Say this prayer with me now:

Dear God, I want you to be my Father; I want to be a follower of Jesus.

I ask you to come into my life and flood me with your love and overtake me with your grace. Forgive me for ignoring you and setting you aside. I give you my future from now, in Jesus' Name.

Amen

If you have prayed this prayer, you are about to experience overwhelming love and freedom that is to be enjoyed to the full without guilt or worry. Now, ask Holy Spirit to fill you with joy and to direct you to a family of other Christ followers who can help you.

Also please contact me and let me know you have done this. I will pray for you and help you any way I am able.

Oceans – Where my Feet May Wander

Spirit lead me where my trust is without borders,
   Let me walk upon the waters,
   Wherever You would call me
   Take me deeper than my feet could ever wander,
   And my faith will be made stronger
   In the presence of my Saviour.

You call me out upon the waters,
   The great unknown where feet may fail,
   And there I find You in the mystery
   In oceans deep, My faith will stand.

And I will call upon Your name
   And keep my eyes above the waves.
   When oceans rise, my soul will rest in Your embrace
   For I am Yours and You are mine.

Your grace abounds in deepest waters,
   Your sovereign hand, Will be my guide.
   Where feet may fail and fear surrounds me
   You've never failed and You won't start now.

So I will call upon Your name
   And keep my eyes above the waves.
   When oceans rise, my soul will rest in Your embrace
   For I am Yours and You are mine.

I will call upon Your name,
   Keep my eyes above the waves,
   My soul will rest in Your embrace,
   I am Yours and You are mine.

Hillsong United

Epilogue

Where Are We Now?

It is 9.22am on Thursday March 8, 2018 and my husband and I, though still living separately, are preparing our future together.

We go on holiday in two weeks, then the plan is to begin the process of building and cementing our married life;

Living under the same roof, sharing the same address and fastening all the other areas of our lives to one another for the rest of our lives.

Planning the dream...nothing but the dream...

It was two years seven months ago when our life as everyone knew it fell apart. At our first counselling session it was pointed out to us that it would take at least three years for my husband to break free from his addictions and sever the attachments that were consequential to his habitual practices.

This is due to the "Cycle of Change" that happens with any addiction. A qualified counsellor explained this to me recently and it helped me to understand the "topsy-turvy" life we lived, most poignantly, the past few years.

The cycle is...

Pre-contemplation, contemplation, action, relapse and action.

I am not ready to thank whoever it was that exposed my husband as it was a vile act, but it brought us to rock bottom and the only way from there is up.

To climb back up takes time and courage and it is tough.

Only our Father in Heaven knows when we will reach the top.

We haven't seen this cliff face before and we don't know where it will lead.

I expect it to be better than anywhere we have been before.

I am a shameless optimist, which is better than the alternative.

I have never given up hope on my marriage, even in the darkest of days when hope was dim, deep in my heart the bond was strong.

I have experienced God's strong arms of love, protection and guidance powerfully through this season of turmoil. He is my goal, He has ordered my steps and I am confident He will complete His purposes whatever they are and look like.

Our union and marriage has been tested beyond human capacity to survive. Though I always knew we were "solid" there were times I wondered if it was our vocation in Christian Leadership that kept us strong, and without it we would not "fit" together.

It appears now all is lost we both still love each other very much. We enjoy each other's company and we are good mates, and all the old jokes are shared with affection, a smile and a look in our eyes.

> *No trust —*
> *No dream*

To date 6.30pm on Thursday April 5, two days after our thirty-sixth wedding anniversary, my husband has relapsed, retreated again into the one that messes with my head and causes me to question my senses. It is proved that my husband is unable to continue in reconciliation. He is unable to trust himself to remain true and faithful.

He cannot be the two characters at the same time anymore, and is unable to disassociate. So he flies from one to the other because he is still both of them, this is who he is, while his pain and loss remain locked inside of him.

Epilogue

One day, I hope he will win the war.

For that to happen one of him must die.

Like conjoined twins where a decaying one will eventually kill the healthier one; for the one to live, the other must be cut away and perish.

Until then, the dream can wait ~ is it still a *YES but not YET?*

For now, I am thankful for every day ~ to embrace every moment.

The Way of Love from 1 Corinthians 13 *The Message Bible*

> Love never gives up,
> Love always cares for others more than self,
> Love isn't always "me first"
> Love doesn't keep score of the sins of others,
> Love always trusts,
> Love never looks back,
> Love keeps going to the end ~ Love never dies.
> For now, we have three things to do;
> Trust steadily in God,
> Hope unswervingly and
> Love extravagantly.

The best of the three is *LOVE.*

Reverend Grey

From the One Born of Fire – Gift of God

*R*everend Grey has been the most challenging book I have ever read, mainly because it catalogues much of my life with all its twists and turns, joy and hurt, love and deceit.

Compartmentalising and disassociating from my actions was the way I kept a double life separate and inexcusably failed, despite numerous attempts, to leave the grey areas of deception and walk in the light of the truth and love offered.

Since being exposed the shame, guilt and engulfing darkness has been a torment to live with despite the best attempts of godly counsellors, a wife and friends who would not let me go.

My hope in supporting my wife in her writing with such fearless honesty is to help anyone who connects in any way shape or form with our story, to show the courage we failed to and uncover the wounds or deceit sooner rather than later to someone you trust or a professional counsellor. In doing that you will help to protect yourself, family and friends from the hurt, bewilderment and shame that comes from uncontrollable exposure and begin as soon as possible a journey of repentance and reconciliation that brings healing and freedom.

It's time to set aside the pressures of 'what if' and start to experience the sweet freedom of an authentic life!

It is my hope and desire to do everything I can to make life better than expected for the future of my marriage and family.

Phil

From the Children...

Reading this book has been somewhat of an emotional roller coaster. While nothing I read was "new news", to me seeing it in print gave me time to process some of the news.

It is, of course, impossible for my brothers and I to be anything but subjective as we process what is our parents' story.

From the offset my anger and disappointment was directed toward my father. As I read about my young mother pacing the living room gone midnight wondering where on earth her husband is, discovering letters and noticing his suspicious behaviour, I place myself in her shoes and I can only imagine the hurt.

However, as I continued to read the book I found I was increasingly angry with my mother. Angry at her for her silence, at her decision not to remove herself from the situation and yet continue to say "why has he done this again?" "How far will he take this?" I found myself saying, in a rather raised voice, "THEN LEAVE MOTHER!!!!"

My brothers and I knew nothing of my dad's problems and my mother's anxieties when we were growing up, we were shielded from much of the dysfunction, although looking back it is easy to put the pieces together and understand some things that we hadn't before.

Now, looking back on our childhood it is difficult to not feel like it was just papier-mâché; put your fist through it and it's flattened.

Moving forward, only time will tell. It will need more than just words of promise but action followed by more action.

All we can do is give it time and hope for a better future for them both.

Appendix

Theories of attachment

Bowlby's Theory: Every child is born with an inbuilt need for at least one key attachment, this person is generally the child's mother and will be more important than any other attachment they make and the attachment a child makes with their mother is unique (www.simple psychology.org).

John Bowlby (1907-1990) British Child Psychiatrist & Psychoanalyst. He was the first attachment theorist, describing attachment as a "lasting psychological connectedness between human beings". Bowlby believed that the earliest bonds formed by children with their caregivers have a tremendous impact that continues throughout life. According to Bowlby, attachment also serves to keep the infant close to the mother, thus improving the child's chances of survival.

Mary Ainsworth: Her theory derived from a demonstration with children their caregivers and strangers, watching and observing the behaviour of children with their caregivers in different scenarios. She found that children with secure attachments became anxious when their caregivers leave them, and found comfort when they came to them when stressed. Children who had insecure attachments didn't find comfort from their caregiver when they were upset, and didn't have the 'secure base' that children with secure attachments have.

NSPCC Survey – Online Porn Survey
Children and young people are now able to access porn online very easily.
Childline (a free 24-hour counselling service for children and young people up to their 19th birthday in the UK provided by the NSPCC), has seen a 6% increase in counselling sessions where the young person specifically mentioned concerns about online porn or websites containing harmful content. (NSPCC, 2015)

Reverend Grey

Concerns related to addiction and worries about forming relationships in the future:

Boy, 12-15:"I'm always watching porn and some of it is quite aggressive. I didn't think it was affecting me at first but I've started to view girls a bit differently recently. I would like to get married in the future but I'm scared it might never happen if I carry on thinking about girls the way I do."

Studies have also shown that when children and young people are exposed to sexually explicit material, they are at greater risk of developing:

- Unrealistic attitudes about sex and consent
- More negative attitudes towards roles and identities in relationships
- More casual attitudes towards sex and sexual relationships
- An increase in 'risky' sexual behaviour
- Unrealistic expectations of body image and performance.

Three in four young women believe porn has led to pressure on women to act a certain way.

Imogen Parker (2014) Young people, sex and relationships: the new norms (PDF).

https://www.nspcc.org.uk/preventing-abuse/keeping-children-safe/online-porn/

References

- Kühn, S. and Gallinat, J. (2014) Brain structure and functional connectivity associated with pornography consumption: the brain on porn. JAMA Psychiatry, 71(7): 827-34.
- NSPCC (2015) "Always there when I need you": ChildLine review: what's affected children in April 2014 - March 2015. London: NSPCC.
- Voon V., Mole T.B., Banca P., Porter L., Morris L., et al. (2014) Neural correlates of sexual cue reactivity in individuals with and without compulsive sexual behaviours. PLoS ONE, 9(7).

Trauma Induced Sex Addiction

Trauma can be induced as a result of childhood abuse, assault or an

Appendix

extended period of stress and anxiety such as, the loss of a parental figure and witnessing domestic violence. The NSPCC defines abuse as:
Emotional abuse as an "undermining of a child's confidence and sense of self-worth" resulting in low self-esteem shame and a reduced ability to care for self and others. When abuse happened within the family of origin there will almost certainly also be attachment issues.
The earlier the trauma the more significant the effect on the brain. It is now known that the imprint of significant early trauma is in the limbic system and in the brain stem – stored in our primitive animal brain not our thinking brain. The amygdala responsible for our 'fight or flight' response remains hypersensitive long after the trauma has gone.
The repetitive nature of compulsive sexual behaviour can be a way for the trauma sufferer to numb feelings of hyperarousal such as hyperactivity, obsessive thinking, and panic along with rage at the lack of protection.
Sex may also be used to alleviate feelings of disassociation, numbness, depression and exhaustion. (Fowler 2006, Fisher 2007) Sex may have become a means of self-soothing or a way of self-harming reinforcing a sense of worthlessness and isolation.
Someone with attachment induced addiction will be unconsciously using their behaviour as a means of soothing pain such as fear of rejection, suffocation loneliness or low-self-esteem. The sexual behaviour may be a way of getting close to others in a controlled manner without true intimacy or alternatively a way of creating or maintaining distance from an otherwise committed relationship.
There is no readily available adequate education or advice and no public health warning of the negative consequences of acting out your desires and fantasies you may think it harmless joy - until of course you are hooked.
Adolescence is a particularly vulnerable phase of development to the suggestive influence of porn. The teenager's task is to successfully negotiate the journey of developing self-identity. It is a time of change and experimentation looking to peers for advice and affirmation rather than parents. Teens often report feeling

249

different from their peers lonely and shy. These differences isolate the individual further making it easier, if opportunity is available to seek solace in porn and masturbation creating a sense of shame and further alienation from friends and potential partners. High levels of pornography viewing by teens negatively affects this critical developmental phase teenagers ordinarily go through in order to learn how to explore their sexuality in a healthy way and creates lower levels of sexual self-esteem. And so the stage is set for addiction.

Pleasure is a physical process not purely psychological; triggered primarily by dopamine endorphins (natural opioids) and adrenaline -: chemicals in our brains. While different sexual experiences trigger different chemicals dopamine in particular is responsible for our reward and pleasure experience. The sex addict by their behaviour has developed a fast access route to the source of these pleasure chemicals which can be stimulated by anticipation fantasy and having sex. (Crenshaw 1996)

The problem is among the literally millions of neuro pathways in our brain if we always access these pleasure pathways in the same way, they will become stronger and other pathways previously used to access the pleasure chemicals will become weaker. These pathways become less effective and the addict finds they need more stimulation in order to get the same affect. (Blum et al. 2000) As the addict seeks increased stimulation to receive the same excitement, crossing boundaries into illegal behaviour poses a real threat. 43 per cent reported viewing either child or animal pornography and 18 per cent had engaged in exhibitionist or voyeuristic behaviours (Hall, 2012)

http://www.kacp.co.uk/phdi/p1.nsf/supppages/5862?opendocumen t&part=10

Survey from *Premier Christianity* magazine, June 2016
42% of UK Christian men admit 'porn addiction'
The stats:
30% Church leaders who access porn on the Internet more than once a month
42% Christian men who say they have a 'porn addiction'

Appendix

90% Christians who believe the Church does not adequately support those who struggle with pornography use
75% Christian men who view pornography on a monthly or less regular basis
10% Christian men who say they have paid for sex
Of those who took part in the survey many called on the Church to rethink the way it addresses the issue of pornography.
One respondent said: "Churches just need to talk about this more often, and straight up ask men individually: 'Do you look at porn?' You'll get much better results in winning the war on porn with that."
https://www.premier.org.uk/News/UK/42-of-UK-Christian-men-admit-porn-addiction

Article in the Daily Mirror highlighting the problems Pornography was having on young men, August 2016
Online porn addiction is causing a rise in erectile dysfunction in young men
Males in their late teens and early 20s are being 'de-sensitised' by graphic videos, leaving them unable to get aroused in the bedroom
An increasing number of young men are seeking treatment for erectile dysfunction normally associated with the middle-aged - because of their addiction to online porn.
Frequent exposure to graphic images and films is de-sensitising men in their late teens and early 20s.
The problem is being exacerbated by the proliferation of smartphones and tablets, which are making pornography immediately accessible.
A new US study in the Behavioural Sciences Journal claims that online porn mirrors drug-like addiction qualities, leading to lowered sexual "enjoyment" and diminished limbo.
The report adds: "The potential health risks of internet pornography are not as well understood as those for alcohol and tobacco use, and (it) is widely portrayed as both ordinary behaviour and socially acceptable."
http://www.mirror.co.uk/news/uk-news/online-porn-addiction-causing-rise-8636996
Josh McDowell Ministries and Covenant Eyes – US Survey

January 2016
The most up-to-date statistics – Ron DeHaas January 2016
Josh McDowell Ministries and Covenant Eyes have commissioned the Barna Group to do a major study in the US on pornography, called *The Porn Phenomenon*. Based on a survey of 3288 people, we now have up-to-date, accurate statistics on many aspects of pornography use, attitudes about pornography, and demographically sorted differences based on age, gender, and faith.
Accountability works: Results for Covenant Eyes users
Addictive nature of porn: Among users of porn, only 55% of general population adults think porn is "definitely" addictive; 94% of Covenant Eyes users think so.
Sexting: Covenant Eyes teens and young adults are 1/3 as likely to have sent a nude image over the Internet.
Recommended: More than 3/4 of youth pastors recommend accountability software as a resource for those who struggle with porn, and believe it is effective.
Generational differences
• When asked to prioritize what people consider to be immoral, adults put "not recycling" pretty near the bottom of their list. Teens and young adults, however, consider "not recycling" to be more immoral than viewing pornography!
• 22% of young adults aged 18 to 24 consider porn to be good for society. 8% of that age group actually think it is "very good for society." Nobody over age 50 thought so.
• The 18 to 24-year-old group is more likely than any other age group actively to seek out porn (57% at least monthly). Meanwhile, over 70% of those over 50 say the "never" actively seek out porn.
Increase in porn use = decrease in sensitivity to porn
While there is no cause and effect relationship, it is clear that people who use porn are more likely to think it's fine to do so – with the exception of Covenant Eyes users, pastors, evangelical Christians, and many people over 50.
• Data from *The Porn Phenomenon* shows that the definition of pornography is much different today than it was in the days of Ricky and Lucy sleeping in separate beds with their

pajamas on. An image of sexual intercourse is NOT pornography to 21% of adults. A fully nude image that is sexually arousing is NOT pornography to 47% of adults. A fully nude image is NOT pornography to 76% of adults.

- Only about 50% of respondents under age 50 who use pornography think that sexual images are "always wrong" if they portray sexual acts that may be forced or painful.
- Only about 40% of respondents under age 50 who use pornography thought that sexual images are "always wrong" if the images are of someone being depicted in a demeaning way. Common examples of demeaning images are women wearing dog collars and leashes being led by their masters and even eating and drinking from dog dishes. Other images show women with foul and obscene labels written on their bodies, or in some cases tattooed on their bodies. And it really is much worse, but not fit for this writing. How can 40% of any civilized society think that's OK?

Differences between faith groupings:
- More than 80% of pastors say that an image that is sexually arousing is porn. Only about half (53%) of general population adults think so. Makes me wonder about the other 20% of pastors...
- 73% of pastors feel at least somewhat equipped to deal with pornography when someone comes to them for help. But only 7% of churches have any programme whatsoever.
- 64% of youth pastors and 57% of pastors struggled with pornography currently or in the past. 54% of youth pastors who currently struggle "live in constant fear of being discovered." 41% of adult Christians think pastors should resign if they are found using porn; only 8% of pastors think so. No wonder they live in constant fear!

http://www.covenanteyes.com/2016/01/19/what-are-the-most-up-to-date-stats-on-pornography/

Reverend Grey

254

Other Resources and Reading

Naked Truth Project aims to open eyes and free lives from the damaging impact of pornography. Through their education, awareness and recovery programmes they help men, women, teenagers, parents and pastors navigate the issue of pornography. Whether you're looking for help to stop your porn-use, or want to learn more about the impact of pornography, the team at *Naked Truth Project* would love to hear from you.
nakedtruthproject.com

Click to Kick is *Naked Truth Project's* recovery and accountability programme. It's an eight week online support group for men and women wanting to overcome porn use and dependency. *Click to Kick* is a course using professional tried and tested models and methods. Developed by one of the UK's leading experts in porn addiction, *Click to Kick* will give you the tools and support you need to find freedom from porn.
clicktokick.com

Confronting Porn **by Paula Hall** is a biblical and practical approach to the issue of porn, offering hope and support for individuals struggling with porn and those who want to help them. In a new landscape where porn has never been more accessible, anonymous or potentially addictive, this book is a timely response for Christians seeking principles and proven steps towards freedom.
Available from: **nakedtruthresources.com**

Footholds and Strongholds: Discerning and Destroying the Work of the Enemy

Pornography is just one area in which the enemy seeks to exercise destructive influence and control in people's lives. Demonic powers are constantly looking for footholds to build strongholds. They can operate as negative and destructive thought patterns which are burned into our minds through repetition and traumatic experiences. This book, by international author David Holdaway, will help you to identify where these

footholds and strongholds are and how to demolish them. Even more importantly it will show you how to build godly strongholds in their place.

How to Stand Against a Spiritual Attack

What is the armour of God and how do I wear it? Subjects such as *Overcoming Temptation*, *The Armour of God*, *Hold the High Ground*, *Meeting Trouble Triumphantly* and many other practical topics are explained clearly and powerfully in David Holdaway's book. It will help you recognise the source and strategy of spiritual attacks and even more importantly how to stand against them and overcome them to live a victorious life in Christ.

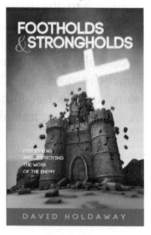

Both available from *Life Publications* at www.lifepublications.org.uk and on Amazon.